LIBRARY OF

MONEY AND BANKING HISTORY

THE CURRENCY OF THE BRITISH COLONIES

THE

CURRENCY

OF THE

BRITISH COLONIES

[JAMES PENNINGTON]

[1848]

REPRINTS OF ECONOMIC CLASSICS

AUGUSTUS M. KELLEY · PUBLISHERS
NEW YORK · 1967

First Edition 1848

(London: Clowes & Co., *Stamford Street*, 1848
FOR HER MAJESTY'S STATIONERY OFFICE)

Reprinted 1967 by
AUGUSTUS M. KELLEY PUBLISHERS

Library of Congress Catalogue Card Number

67 - 18578

PRINTED IN THE UNITED STATES OF AMERICA

THE

CURRENCY

OF THE

BRITISH COLONIES.

LONDON:

PRINTED BY W. CLOWES AND SONS, STAMFORD STREET,

FOR HER MAJESTY'S STATIONERY OFFICE.

M DCCC XLVIII.

CONTENTS.

INTRODUCTION.

PREVIOUSLY to the year 1838, the metallic money of the British colonies was in a confused and unsatisfactory state, and peremptorily required the interference of the Government. Conflicting coins and conflicting money denominations were the perpetual source of difficulty and complaint, both with respect to the domestic traffic of the colonies, and their external commerce. The standard to which those denominations referred, was not distinctly fixed by law; and the meaning and intention of pecuniary contracts were, consequently, in many cases, equivocal and uncertain. Coins of gold and silver were not accurately adjusted to each other. Those of the former metal were generally over-valued with respect to those of the latter; and this over-valuation rendered it extremely difficult to retain in circulation coins of the inferior metal in a sound and perfect state, and in sufficient quantity for the business of domestic interchange.

The currency of the colonies consisted principally of Spanish and Portuguese coins, current at nominal rates established by law or custom.*

In the application of those rates to British and foreign coins, the monetary denominations of the parent state were adopted. They were, however, differently applied in different colonies. In Canada, for example, the rate assigned to the British shilling was one shilling and one penny; to the Spanish dollar, five shillings; and to the Spanish doubloon, three pounds four shillings; while in Jamaica, the same coins were rated as follows:—

	£.	s.	d.
British shilling . . .	0	1	8
Spanish dollar . . .	0	6	8
Spanish doubloon . .	5	6	8

It thus appears that not only were different rates assigned to the same coins in different colonies, but the rates assigned were proportionately different with reference to the intrinsic value of the different coins.

* The use of those coins as the medium of interchange in the British colonies in the West Indies and America, naturally arose from the contiguity of those colonies to the countries which are in possession of the mines, from which supplies of gold and silver are transmitted to the rest of the world, chiefly in the form of coins.

To this practice no reasonable objection could be made. In the principal countries of Europe, the establishment of Mints has, indeed, rendered national coins the peculiar medium of interchange in those countries; yet some states have risen to great wealth and commercial distinction, without adopting the principle of an exclusive coinage. England and France have maintained the exclusive system; but Holland, Hamburgh, Genoa, and the United States of America, have, with greater or less freedom, received, and permitted the circulation of the coins of Mints of established reputation, at rates corresponding to their intrinsic values, without suffering from this practice any detriment or inconvenience.

In order to apply a safe and effectual remedy to those discrepancies, and rightly to adjust the rates assigned to British and foreign coins relatively to each other, it became necessary to consider, first, the state of the law under which the coinage and currency of the metallic money of Great Britain are regulated; and, secondly, the circumstances which gradually led to the establishment of our present gold standard, and to the use of silver tokens as a subsidiary and subordinate currency.

First. The state of the law.

The right to declare the rate or value at which coins of gold and silver shall pass current and be a legal tender, is a branch of the Royal prerogative, which the sovereigns of this realm have from time immemorial enjoyed and exercised.

This right has been distinctly recognised by various statutes. Thus, the 19th of Henry VII. c. 5, enacts, that "all gold and silver coins shall "pass current for the sum they were coined for;" and the 5th & 6th of Edward VI. c. 19, enacts, that "if any person exchanged any coined gold or "coined silver, receiving or paying any more in "value than the same be declared by his Majesty's "proclamation to be current for within his Ma- "jesty's dominions, the same shall be forfeited," and the person so offending be punished as therein directed.

The right of setting a rate or value on the coins authorised to be current, has been exercised in two

different ways. First, by indentures of agreement
with the officers of the Mint; in which indentures
a clause is inserted, declaring the rate or value at
which the coins therein directed to be made shall
pass current; and secondly, by proclamation.

The coins issued from the Mint are held, in all
ordinary cases, to be legally current at the rate or
value assigned to them in the Mint indentures.
When the nominal value of the coin already in
circulation is to be raised or lowered, or when
foreign coins are to be made current at a certain
fixed rate, a proclamation is necessary.*

Although the Royal prerogative, in this respect,
is clear and unquestionable, it must be admitted
that great caution and circumspection are requisite
in the exercise of it; for although equity would
require, and our courts of law would rule,
that if the rates or denominations of the coins
already current were raised or lowered, or if the
quantity of fine gold or silver contained in coins of
a given denomination were increased or lessened, a
contract of debt must be construed, according to
the meaning and intention of the contracting parties at the time it was entered into; and would not
absolve a debtor from his engagement, who offered
to pay his debt with coins of less real value than
those that were legally current when the debt was
contracted; still the difficulty of clearly distinguishing in every case the debts contracted in terms

* Lord Liverpool on the Coins.

of the previous currency, from those contracted in terms of the altered coins, would be attended with great inconvenience, perplexity, and contention.

In the present enlightened state of the public mind on this subject, it is not indeed probable that any serious attempt will be made to alter either the weight, the fineness, or the denominations of the coins already current in Great Britain. In the colonies, however, the case is different; and as the prerogative of the Crown, with respect to the rate or value at which coins shall pass current and be a legal tender, extends to the colonies as well as to the parent state, the Government may properly and usefully interfere to correct any irregularities and imperfections which may still prevail there.

Secondly. The circumstances which led to the establishment of our present gold standard, and the use of subordinate silver coins.

For this purpose it is not necessary to go further back than to the 43rd year of the reign of Queen Elizabeth.

In that year the fineness of silver was restored to the standard of old sterling, namely, 11 oz. 2 dwts. of fine silver, and 18 dwts. of alloy; and a pound, troy weight, of that silver was directed to be coined into sixty-two shillings.

The standard for gold was, at the same time, 22 carats fine, and 2 carats alloy; and a pound, troy weight, of gold of that standard was coined into 33½ sovereigns, and passed current for 33*l.* 10*s.*, each sovereign weighing 7 dwts. 4 grs., and passing current for twenty shillings.

The alterations that were made in the weight of the gold coins, subsequently to that period, appear to have been adopted chiefly with the view of bringing their value in tale to a due proportion with the value of the silver coins, according to the relative value of gold and silver in the market.

Although the value of gold, relatively to silver, was estimated in the 43rd year of the reign of Elizabeth, in a less proportion to silver than in the reign of Edward III., no adjustment of the relative value of the two metals, in the coins, appears to have been required until soon after the beginning of the reign of James I. From that period, the rise in the value of gold, compared with silver, was great and rapid. In the 2nd and 3rd years of the reign of that monarch, the weight of the sovereign, or twenty-shilling piece, was reduced to 6 dwts. 10¾ grs., and by further reductions in the 9th and 17th years of the same reign, the weight of the sovereign, or twenty-shilling piece, was brought down to 5 dwts. 20½ grs.

No further reduction was made in the weight of the gold coins, or in their value relatively to the silver coins, until the 15th year of the reign of Charles II., when the weight of the twenty-shilling piece was reduced from 5 dwts. 20½ grs., to

5 dwts. 9½ grs. This coin was afterwards called a guinea.

It is here proper to state, that, previously to the 15th of Charles II., the gold coins were a legal tender of payment, at the rates established in the Mint indentures; they were afterwards allowed to vary with the variations in the relative value of the two metals in the market.

In the reigns of Charles II. and James II., the silver coins had become greatly deteriorated by wear and clipping. This evil increased so rapidly, that it was found, by experiments made by the officers of the Exchequer in the year 1695, that those coins were defective to the extent of nearly one half of their original weight.* In a report from Mr. Lowndes to the Lords of the Treasury, dated the 12th September of that year, it is stated that " the exchange with the low countries was " fallen so very low, that the public lost about four " shillings in the pound upon all monies remitted " thither—that the exchange to Hamburgh and " the east countries was still lower." He further states, " That the price of silver was risen to 6s. 5d. " per ounce, and the guinea to 30s."

Under these circumstances a recoinage of the silver coins was undertaken, and executed at an expense of about 2,700,000l.

When the recoinage was completed, the guinea, the value of which had been reduced by Act of

* Lord Liverpool on the Coins.

Parliament (7 and 8 William III., c. 10, s. 18) to 22*s.*, became current at 21*s.* 6*d.*, at which rate it was received by the Government in the payment of taxes.* This fall in the value of the guinea was not sufficiently great to bring it to a level with the value of the silver coin. The consequence was, that the new silver coins were melted down and exported; and although 6,882,908*l.* 17*s.* 7*d.* in tale had been coined, the greatest part of this sum, in the course of 18 years, disappeared.†

In this state were the coins of this kingdom in the year 1717, when the Government, alarmed at the great diminution of the silver coins, applied to Sir Isaac Newton, then Master of the Mint, for his advice.

The following are extracts from the Report of Sir Isaac Newton upon that occasion:—

" A pound weight of gold, 11 oz. fine, and 1 oz. alloy,
" is cut into 44½ guineas; and a pound weight of silver,
" 11 oz. 2 dwts. fine, and 18 dwts. alloy, is cut into 62*s.*;
" and, according to this rate, a pound weight of fine gold
" is worth 15 lb. 6 oz. 17 dwts. 5 grs. of fine silver, reck-
" oning a guinea at 21*s.* 6*d.* in silver money. But silver
" in bullion, exportable, is usually worth 2*d.* or 3*d.* per
" ounce more than in coin; and if at a medium, if such

---

* It was proposed by Mr. Locke, that silver should be the only fixed legal standard, and that guineas should pass current at their value in silver. This advice was disregarded; for as guineas were received by the Government in payment of taxes, at the rate of 21*s.* 6*d.*, the effect was nearly the same as if they had been made a legal tender at that rate.

† Lord Liverpool on the Coins.

" bullion of standard alloy be valued at 5s. 4½d. per
" ounce, a pound-weight of fine gold will be worth 14 lb.
" 11 oz. 12 dwts. 9 grs. of fine silver in bullion ; and at
" this rate, a guinea is worth so much silver as would
" make 20s. 8d. When ships are lading for the East
" Indies, the demand for silver for exportation raises the
" price to 5s. 6d. or 5s. 8d. per ounce, or above ; but I
" consider not these extraordinary cases.

" It is the demand for exportation which hath raised
" the price of exportable silver about 2d. or 3d. in the
" ounce above that of silver in coin, and hath thereby
" created a temptation to export or melt down the silver
" coin, rather than give 2d. or 3d. more for foreign silver ;
" and the demand for exportation arises from the higher
" price of silver in other places than in England in pro-
" portion to gold—that is, from the higher price of gold
" in England than in other places in proportion to silver.
" If gold in England, or silver in East India, could be
" brought down so low as to bear the same proportion to
" one another in both places, there would be here no
" greater demand for silver than for gold to be exported
" to India. And if gold were lowered only so as to have
" the same proportion to silver money in England which
" it hath to the silver money in the rest of Europe, there
" would be no temptation to export silver rather than
" gold to any other part of Europe ; and to compass this
" last, there seems nothing more requisite than to take
" off 10d. or 12d. from the guinea, so that gold may bear
" the same proportion to the silver money in England
" which it ought to do by the course of trade and ex-
" change in Europe. But if only 6d. were taken off at
" present, it would diminish the temptation to export or
" melt down the silver coins, and by the effects would
" show hereafter, better than can appear at present what

" further reduction would be most convenient for the
" publick.

" If things be let alone till money be a little scarcer,
" the gold will fall of itself; for people are already back-
" ward to give silver for gold, and will in a little time
" refuse to make payments in silver without a premium,
" as they do in Spain, and this premium will be an abate-
" ment in the value of gold; and so the question is,
" whether gold shall be lowered by the Government,
" or let alone till it falls of itself by the want of silver
" money."

In pursuance of the advice given by that great
man, the value of the guinea was lowered by proclamation to 21s., and other gold coins in proportion.

Upon that occasion the Government departed
from the principle adopted in the 7th and 8th of
William III.

Previously to the passing of that Act, the guinea
was allowed to be exchanged at any rate above the
rate set forth in the Mint indentures.

The 7th and 8th William III. prohibited the
currency of that coin at any higher rate than 26s.,
and afterwards at any higher rate than 22s.; but
in the proclamation issued by King George I., it
was expressly declared that " the said respective
" pieces of coined gold shall be current at the
" rates set upon them."

After the publication of this proclamation, the
rate at which the guinea passed current could no
longer vary with the variations in the relative value

of gold and silver in the market, but was permanently fixed at 21s.

The alterations that have been made in the value of the gold coins relatively to silver, are exhibited in the following tabular statement :—

Reign.	A.D.	Weight of 20s. in Tale of Silver.			Weight of 20s. in Tale of Gold.		Proportion of fine Gold to fine Silver.
		Oz.	Dwts.	Grs.	Dwts.	Grs.	
43 Elizabeth,	1601	3	17	$10\frac{2}{31}$	7	4	10·905
2 & 3 James I.	1606	3	17	$10\frac{2}{31}$	6	$10\frac{3}{4}$	12·109
9 James I.	1612	3	17	$10\frac{2}{31}$	5	$20\frac{15}{22}$	13·320
17 James I.	1619	3	17	$10\frac{2}{31}$	5	$20\frac{1}{2}$	13·346
15 Charles II.	1663	3	17	$10\frac{2}{31}$	5	$9\frac{1}{2}$	13·485
3 George I.	1717	3	17	$10\frac{2}{31}$	5	3	15·209

It appears from the foregoing statement, that from the 43rd of Elizabeth to the 15th of Charles II., the rise in the value of gold with respect to silver, as estimated in the coins, was gradual and progressive. In the changes that were successively made, the value of gold, however, except during a short interval in the reign of James II., was certainly overrated. The Mint proportions differed from the market proportions. The rate or value assigned to the gold coins with respect to those of silver, was higher than it ought to have been. The consequence was, that the silver coins were melted down and exported, and the principal importation into the Mint was gold.

Thus, during nearly the whole of the period above-mentioned, gold became the predominant metal in the currency, and the principal measure of property and exchange.

It has already been observed, that the greatest part of the silver coins fabricated in the reign of King William III. had, in the course of 18 years, been melted down and exported.

In his treatise on the coins of the realm, published in the year 1805, Lord Liverpool states that the nominal value of the silver coins which were coined in that reign, and those which had occasionally been coined since that period, amounted to 8,076,092*l.*, and that of those, the whole of the crown-pieces, and a moiety of the half-crowns, had disappeared. The total value of the legal silver coins in circulation in 1798, he estimated at about 3,900,000*l.*, of which the deficiency in weight was found, by experiments made by the officers of the Mint, to be as follows :—

$$\text{Half-crowns} \quad 3\tfrac{1}{3}\tfrac{6}{1}\tfrac{1}{3} \text{ per cent.}$$
$$\text{Shillings} \quad 24\tfrac{1}{3}\tfrac{9}{2}\tfrac{6}{0}\tfrac{4}{9} \text{ per cent.}$$
$$\text{Sixpences} \quad 38\tfrac{2}{8}\tfrac{2}{0}\tfrac{9}{3}\tfrac{4}{7} \text{ per cent.}$$

The deficiency in the weight of the silver coins, when the general re-coinage of the gold coins, which commenced in 1774, was completed, was probably not much less than the deficiency above described.

In that year, the Act of the 14 Geo. III., c. 42, was passed. By that Act, the silver coins were ordered to be a legal tender for sums exceeding twenty-five pounds, only according to their weight, at the rate of 5*s.* 2*d.* per ounce. That Act expired in 1783, and was not renewed till 1798, so that in the intervening period, a debt of any amount might have been legally discharged with six-pences, wanting upwards of thirty per cent. of their original weight.

It may here be observed, that the enactments above-mentioned were, in every respect, nugatory, inasmuch as no one could avail himself of the per-mission to pay a debt in light silver coins by weight without serious loss. If, for example, the shillings were deficient to the extent of 20 per cent. of their original weight, 2500 of those shil-lings, or 125*l.* in tale, would have been required, under this regulation, to discharge a debt of one hundred pounds. It is true, indeed, that before the year 1798, it was competent to any one to bring silver to the Mint to be coined, and thus to discharge his money obligations with silver, at the rate of 5*s.* 2*d.* per ounce; but as at that time the price of silver was higher in the market than at the Mint, no one, without considerable disadvan-tage, could avail himself of the privilege.

In the year 1798, the price of silver had so far fallen, as to induce some individuals to bring that metal to the Mint to be coined at the rate of 5*s.* 2*d.* per ounce.

If that coinage had been permitted to proceed, the gold coins would, in their turn, have been melted down and exported, and the integer, or pound sterling, have become 3 oz. 17 dwts. $10\frac{2}{3}\frac{}{1}$ grs. of silver, instead of 5 dwts. 3·274 grs. of gold. The standard and basis of the currency would have become silver at 5s. 2d. per ounce; and gold would, in no long time, have been banished from the circulation.

In order to prevent this consequence, the 38 Geo. III., c. 59, was passed, by which the further coinage of silver was suspended.

In 1816, the 56 Geo. III., c. 68, was passed, by which it is enacted, that after a day to be appointed by proclamation, silver coin and bullion may be brought to the Mint to be coined, at the rate of 66s. per lb. troy weight; and that the silver so coined shall be a legal tender to the extent of forty shillings.

The 9th section of this Act gives reason to suppose that it was originally intended by the Government to open the Mint to the public for the coinage of silver, at the rate therein mentioned, and to retain 4s. per lb., as seignorage, relying upon the limitation of the legal tender to forty shillings for the prevention of any inconvenient interference with the gold coins; but as no proclamation, to the effect stated in the Act, has been published, the public are precluded from the privilege of bringing silver to the Mint for coinage; and none has been coined since the passing of the Act, without the express permission and authority of the Government.

There is then, at present, no Mint price of silver; none, at least, in the sense in which that expression is commonly understood. The Government purchases silver at the market price, and coins each pound, troy weight, of that silver into sixty-six shillings. By issuing no greater quantity of those coins than is necessary for the purpose of change, their value is sustained on a level with that of the gold coins, according to the proportionate rates and denominations assigned to each. The limitation of the legal tender to forty shillings would not, alone, be sufficient for that purpose; nor would that limitation, if the Mint were open to the public for the coinage of silver in the way and on the conditions stated in the Act, prevent an inconvenient inundation of silver coins. At present the gold price of silver is about 5s. per ounce. At present then, if the Mint were open, a profit of between 3 and 4 per cent. on the coinage of silver would accrue to the importer. Such a profit, although obtainable only on sums of forty shillings at one time, would, if frequently repeated, be a sufficient inducement to money dealers to exchange gold coins for silver bullion, and to force into circulation an undue quantity of coins of the latter metal.

Nor would the charge of a high seignorage prevent this consequence; for the coins delivered at the Mint would still, by law, be of the same exchangeable value as that of the silver which the importer brought there. It would not, otherwise, be brought to the Mint.

The limitation of the amount put into circulation

is then the principal, if not the only cause of the excess of the value of the silver coins over that of the metal of which they are made.

The most eminent writers on coins and money have agreed in the opinion, that the current coin, which is intended to be the principal measure of property, should be made of one metal only. Mr. Locke was of opinion, not only that the principal measure of property should be made of one metal only, but that " silver, for many " reasons, is the fittest of all metals to be this " measure, and, therefore, generally made use of " as money." He, at the same time, thought that " it is necessary your gold should be coined, " and have the King's stamp upon it, to secure " men, in receiving it, that there is so much gold in " each piece ; but it is not necessary that it should " have a fixed rate set on it by publick authority. " It is not convenient that it should, in its varying " proportion, have a settled price. Let gold, as " other commodities, find its own rate, and when " by the King's image and inscription it carries " with it a publick assurance of its weight and " fineness, the gold money, so coined, will never " fail to pass at the known market rates, as readily " as any other species of money."

Mr. Harris was likewise of opinion that the standard measure of commerce should consist of one metal only, and that silver is the fittest material for money; yet he thought that " it may be " very useful to coin gold, to ascertain its fineness, " and to let these coins pass, in lieu of money, at " some given rate."

Upon this point Mr. Harris seems to have fallen into some inaccuracy. He was aware of the impossibility of maintaining in circulation coins of both metals at certain fixed rates, unless the value of the two metals, with respect to each other in the market, should continue the same as the proportionate rates assigned to them at the Mint; and yet he thought (contrary to the opinion of Mr. Locke) that gold coins should not be left to find their own value, without having any established legal rates; that " this is a matter of too " much importance to be left to private judgment, " and if left at large, might subject the nation in " general to great impositions by a combination of " the dealers in coins."

Now, if in the year 1758, when Mr. Harris's " Essay on Money and Coins" was published, it had been determined to establish silver as the principal measure of property, and the instrument of exchange, and at the same time to set a fixed rate or value on the gold coins, it would have been necessary to assign to the guinea a lower rate with reference to the silver coins, than the proportion which gold bore to silver in the market, and to have allowed the gold coins to pass current, at any rate above that minimum rate; in other words, to have allowed the gold coins to bear an agio, or premium, in the market, as against the silver coins.

But this would have really amounted to the same thing as the proposal of Mr. Locke; for as, under such a regulation, no one would part with his gold coins at the minimum rate, the assignment of such a rate would have been nugatory and useless. The gold coins would have been merely pieces, having the King's image and inscription on them to certify their weight and fineness, as proposed by Mr. Locke, and would have passed, in currency, at their known market rates or value.

In this way only, indeed, that is, by allowing gold coins to find their value in the market, can silver, practically, be made the basis of the currency, and the standard to which all money contracts, expressed in terms of that currency, have reference.

Mr. Harris says, that " silver coin is, and time " immemorial hath been, the money of accompt of " the greatest part of the world, and where it is so, " silver is the standard measure of commerce. " And although it be supposed that with us, more " payments are made in gold than in silver coins, " yet that doth not alter the standard whilst the " accompts are kept in silver." He asks, " Is not " a declaration that a guinea shall pass for twenty- " one shillings a plain reference to shillings as a " standard of the value of a guinea?"

It may be so; but at the date of his Essay on

Money the reference here spoken of was merely nominal. The over-valuation of gold, with respect to silver, at the Mint, had long rendered gold, practically, the principal measure of commerce, not only among merchants, but likewise in the business of domestic interchange and traffic. The denomination of twenty-one shillings which had formerly been applied to 4 oz. 1 dwt. 7 grs. of silver, was at that time applied to 5 dwts. $9\frac{1}{2}$ grs. of gold; and when a contract was made for the payment of twenty shillings, 20-21 parts of 5 dwts. $9\frac{1}{2}$ grs. of gold were alone in the contemplation of the contracting parties.

The views of Lord Liverpool, with respect to the standard of money, were different from those of Mr. Locke and Mr. Harris. His Lordship was of opinion that " In very rich countries, where " great and extensive commerce is carried on, " gold is the most proper metal of which the " principal measure of property, and instrument " of commerce, should be made. In such coun-" tries gold will, in practice, become the principal " measure of property, and the instrument of " commerce, with the general consent of the peo-" ple, not only without the support of law, but in " spite of almost any law that may be enacted to " the contrary; for the principal purchases and " exchanges cannot there be made in coins of a " less valuable metal."

Although the utmost deference is justly due to this high authority, it may reasonably be doubted whether the inferences contained in the foregoing passage are, in every respect, correct. It is certain, at least, that if silver, with respect to gold, be estimated at the Mint higher than in the market, and coins of both metals be made a legal tender at the rates fixed in the Mint indentures, then—however extensive and multifarious may be the commerce of the country—no gold will be brought by the public to the Mint to be coined, and the basis of the currency will be silver. It is true that gold has long been the principal measure of property in this country; not, however, as Lord Liverpool imagined, without the support of law, but because, previously to the year 1798, the law had made gold the cheapest tender of payment; and because, since that period, the silver department of the Mint has been closed to the public, and accessible only to the Government.

Lord Liverpool, equally with Mr. Locke and Mr. Harris, thought that the principal measure of property should be made of one metal only; and having come to the conclusion that gold is the most proper metal for that purpose, it became necessary for him to consider in what way silver coins might be provided for small payments without unduly interfering with the gold coins.

It is justly observed by Mr. Harris, in his Essay on Money and Coins, that " there must be coins

" of the value of shillings and sixpences. Those
" sorts of coins are the most frequently wanted ;
" and there is no doing without them, or some
" substitute in their stead. A coin of a shilling,
" or even of half-a-crown value, would be much
" too small for gold." Hence he thought that
gold is much too valuable a metal for the standard of money. He thought, moreover, that, " it
" would be a ridiculous and even vain attempt to
" make a standard integer of gold, whose parts
" should be silver ; or to make a motley standard,
" part gold and part silver."

Lord Liverpool conceived that this difficulty
might be got over by limiting the legal-tender of
the silver coins to the value of single pieces of the
gold coin ; and by establishing the same relation
between the silver coins and copper. He observes,
that " where the function of gold coins as a stand-
" ard measure of property ceases, there that of
" silver coin should begin; and that where the
" function of silver coin, in this respect, ceases,
" there that of copper should begin : it is clear,
" therefore, that so far only these silver and cop-
" per coins should be made legal tender, and no
" further, at least not in any degree; and it fol-
" lows, that the coins, both of silver and copper,
" are subordinate, subservient, and merely repre-
" sentative coins, and must take their value with
" reference to the gold coins, according to the rate
" which the sovereign sets upon each of them."

He further observes, that "the metal of which "these silver coins are made should be estimated, "not according to the actual price of such metal, "but according to the average price which such "metal has borne for a certain number of years "past, or which it is likely to bear, in future, in "the market."

But surely the difficulty would not be overcome in this way. So long as the prices of gold and silver at the Mint are accurately adjusted to the relative value of the two metals in the market, both metals will, indeed, be brought by the public to the Mint to be coined. But if the gold price of silver should rise materially above the Mint price, nobody will bring silver to the Mint; for to do so would, in that case, be attended with certain loss to the importer of the silver, and a scarcity of silver coins would be experienced.

If, on the other hand, the gold price of silver should fall materially below the Mint price, the limitation of the legal tender to the value of single pieces of the gold coin would not be sufficient to prevent an inconvenient importation of silver into the Mint and a redundancy of silver coins.

Lord Liverpool's plan was not adopted; but, as is stated above, the 56th of George III. was passed, by which Act, and the confinement to the Government of the privilege of coining silver at the Mint, the main object of that plan, namely, the issue of a subordinate silver coinage, was successfully accomplished. The basis of the currency is gold 11-12ths fine, and 3*l.* 17*s.* 10½*d.* per ounce. The silver coins are merely subsidiary : the weight and fineness of the latter are matters of little importance : whether a pound weight of silver were coined into sixty-four shillings, sixty-six shillings, or seventy shillings, the value of the coins would not be at all affected ; their value depends, not on the intrinsic worth of the metal of which they are made but on the limitation of their quantity, and the limited amount for which they are a legal tender.

CURRENCY OF THE GOLD AND SILVER COINS OF SPAIN
IN THE BRITISH COLONIES.

In nearly all the colonial possessions of the
Crown, the British denominations of " pounds,
" shillings, and pence," were, at an early period,
adopted in their pecuniary computations and accounts, and are still adhered to.

In the application of those denominations to the
coins which are authorised to pass current, and
which are a legal tender, the practice of the colonies
differs, however, not only from that of the mother
country, but each of the colonies differs, in this respect, from the others. In one place, the denomination of a Spanish dollar is ten shillings ; in another, six shillings and three-pence ; in another,
five shillings.

The inconvenience of this practice appears to
have been felt at an early period. In the sixth
year of the reign of Queen Anne, an Act was
passed, of which the preamble states, that " for
" remedying the inconvenience which has arisen
" from the different rates at which the same species
" of foreign coins did pass in Her Majesty's several
" colonies and plantations in America, Her Most
" Excellent Majesty has thought fit, by Her Royal
" Proclamation, to settle and ascertain the currency
" of foreign coins in Her said colonies and plan-
" tations."

In the proclamation to which this Act refers, it is stated that the principal officers of the Mint had prepared a table of the value of the several coins which usually pass current in the plantations, showing the just proportion which each coin ought to bear to the other; and it is ordained that the currency of all pieces of eight of Peru, dollars, and other foreign species of silver coins, shall stand regulated according, and in proportion, to the rate set for the pieces of eight of Seville, Pillar, and Mexico.

The several species of the Spanish dollar are designated in the proclamation as follows:—

	dwts.	grs.		s.	d.
Seville pieces of eight, old plate .	17	12	=	4	6
Ditto new plate .	14	0	=	3	7¼
Mexico pieces of eight	17	12	=	4	6
Pillar pieces of eight	17	12	=	4	6¾
Peru pieces of eight, old plate . .	17	12	=	4	5
Cross dollars	18	0	=	4	4¾

It is then directed that no Seville, Pillar, or Mexico pieces of eight, though of the full weight of 17½ dwts., shall be accounted for, received, taken, or paid, within any of the colonies or plantations, at above the rate of six shillings per piece, of current money.

At a subsequent period, the wear and mutilation of the coins, the abuse of paper-money, and, probably, the mistaken notion that raising the denomination of coins augments their value, led, in the West Indies and America, to the various systems of currency which now prevail there.

In the proclamation above referred to, it is stated that the inconvenience arising from the different rates at which the same species of foreign coins pass in the several colonies and plantations in America, is the indirect practice of drawing money from one plantation to another, to the great prejudice of Her Majesty's subjects.

This erroneous view probably originated in the false notion that the value of the coins which are made legally current, depends, not merely on their weight and fineness, but, likewise, upon the rates, or denominations, which are, by law, assigned to them.

This notion naturally led to the supposition, that the assignment of a higher rate to any species of coins in one colony over the coins of another, attracted those coins to the favoured colony, to the detriment of its neighbours.

This was an error. The inconvenience, which really resulted from the practice complained of in the proclamation of Queen Anne, was, and still continues to be, not the artificial and forced removal of money from one colony to another, but the troublesome and complex computations and adjustments which are rendered necessary in the operations of the exchange of the colonies with each other, and with the parent state.

If the inconvenience resulting from the assignment of different nominal rates to the same species of coins, in different colonies, were the only ground of complaint, with respect to the currency of those colonies, it might be a question whether it would be worth while to disturb habits and prejudices which have long prevailed, for the sake of that uniformity which it was the object of the proclamation of Queen Anne to accomplish.

Unhappily, another defect, of a more important nature, and more difficult to deal with, long rendered the currency of the colonies unsatisfactory, perplexing, and anomalous. That defect consisted, mainly, in the assignment of disproportionate rates to coins of gold, and coins of silver.

The principal foreign coins current in the colonies are, the gold doubloons, and the silver coins of Spain, Mexico, and South America, and the subdivisions thereof.

According to the monetary regulations of Spain, sixteen dollars are deemed equivalent to one doubloon.

The same proportion was adopted in the British colonies. At Barbadoes, for example, the rate assigned to a gold doubloon was five pounds, and to a silver dollar six shillings and three pence.

This proportionate rate rendered gold the predominant metal in the currency, both of Spain and the West Indies.

In the report of Sir Isaac Newton to the Lords of Her Majesty's Treasury, dated 17th September, 1717, it is stated, that " a Spanish pistole was " coyned for 32 ryalls, or 4 pieces of 8 ryalls, " and is of equal allay, and the sixteenth part of

" the weight thereof; and that this high price
" (that is, the high estimate of gold relatively
" to silver) in Spain, keeps their gold, at home, in
" good plenty, and carries away the Spanish silver
" into all Europe, so that they will not pay in sil-
" ver without a premium."

It is further stated, that " by the course of trade
" and exchange between nation and nation, in all
" Europe, fine gold is to fine silver as 14⅘, or
" 15 to 1."

It thus appears that, at that time, the value of
gold, with respect to silver, was over-rated, or
(which comes to the same thing) the value of silver,
with respect to gold, was under-rated, in the Spanish coinage, to the extent of about 6½ per cent.

Since the date of that report, alterations have
been made in the Mint regulations of Spain, which
alterations, as they have been adopted in the Mints
of Mexico and South America, it is necessary to
notice.

The principal coins of Spain are as follows:—

Of Gold:

	Reals Vellons.
The doubloon of 8 escudos, or quadruple pistole	320
The doubloon de oro, or pistole	80
The Escudo	40
The Coronilla, or Vienlen de oro	20

Of Silver:

The dollar, or pesoduro	20
The half-dollar, or Escudo Vellon	10
The Peceta Mexicana	5

The Peceta Provenceal 4
The Real 2

By the Royal Edict of 1730, $8\frac{1}{2}$ quadruples were to weigh a Castilian mark of gold, of 22 carats fine; and $8\frac{1}{2}$ pesos duros, or dollars, were to weigh a Castilian mark of silver, 11 dineros fine.

Thus, from 1730 to 1772, the gold was 22 carats, and the silver, 11 dineros fine; but, in 1772, the gold was reduced to $21\frac{3}{4}$ carats, and the silver to $10\frac{3}{4}$ dineros fine, except the pecetas and reals, which were reduced to $9\frac{3}{4}$ dineros fine.

No alteration has since taken place in the silver coins; but in 1786, the standard of gold was again reduced to 21 carats for the different doubloons and their divisions, and to $20\frac{3}{8}$ carats for the Coronilla, or Vienlen de oro.*

It thus appears that, according to the monetary and Mint regulations of Spain (the gross weight of a doubloon and of a dollar being the same), the proportion of fine silver to fine gold, previously to the year 1786, was as 16 to 1; and that since 1786, the proportion of fine silver to fine gold has been,

$$\frac{21\cdot5 \times 16}{21} = 16\frac{8}{21} \text{ to } 1.$$

It is here proper to state that, by assays made at Her Majesty's Mint, in the year 1834, the contents of a Mexican, or South American doubloon, were found to be, on an average, 362 grains of fine gold;

* Kelly's Universal Cambist.

and the contents of a dollar, of the same coinage, were found to be, on an average, 373 grains of fine silver, or thereabouts; making the proportion of fine silver to fine gold (reckoning 16 dollars to a doubloon), $16\frac{48}{100}$ to 1.

Although the present proportion of fine silver to fine gold, in the coins of Spain, exceeds the proportion which was shown in the assays made by Sir Isaac Newton, yet that excess has been more than counteracted by the change which has since taken place in the value of silver relatively to gold, in the general market of Europe.

At present, the value of silver, in the general market, is to that of gold in the proportion of about 15·75 to 1, or about $3\frac{1}{2}$ per cent. less than the proportion set in the monetary and Mint regulations of Spain.

This excess of $3\frac{1}{2}$ per cent. in the silver price of gold, at the Spanish Mint, over the general market price of silver, in Europe, is, however, quite sufficient to produce the effect described by Sir Isaac Newton:—"to keep their gold at home, in good " plenty, and to carry away the Spanish silver into " all Europe."

Sir Isaac Newton states some facts in corroboration of his views. It appears that the louis d'or was brought into general circulation in the latter part of King William's reign, from being rated $5\frac{1}{4}d.$ above its value compared with the coins of Great Britain, and that a similar profit of 5d. in

the moidore, inundated the West of England with
those coins.   Upon these facts he observes : " that
" if the advantage of $5\frac{1}{4}d$. in a louis d'or (about $2\frac{1}{2}$
" per cent.) sufficed to bring into England so great
" a quantity of French money, and the advantage
" of three farthings in a louis d'or to bring it to the
" Mint, the advantage of $9\frac{1}{2}d$. in a guinea* may have
" been sufficient to bring in the great quantity of
" gold which hath been coined within the last
" fifteen years, without any foreign silver.   And
" if an advantage of $5d$. in a moidore (about $1\frac{1}{2}$ per
" cent.) did pour that money in upon us, much
" more hath the advantage of $9\frac{1}{2}d$. in a guinea
" been able to bring into the Mint great quantities
" of gold, without any foreign silver, and may be
" able to do so still, till the cause be removed."

* The current value of a guinea was, at that time, over-rated to this
extent, with reference to the relative value of gold and silver in the
market.

THE INTRODUCTION OF THE COINS OF THE MOTHER
COUNTRY INTO THE CURRENCY OF THE COLONIES.

The introduction of the coins of Spain, and of
the Spanish proportions, into the currency of the
British West India islands, was attended with
results similar to those above described. Doubloons were in good plenty in many of the islands,
while dollars were scarce. The difficulty of obtaining small silver coins, in sufficient quantity for
the purpose of domestic traffic, induced the necessity of cutting silver dollars into bits, and the
assignment to those bits of certain nominal rates
in the currency of the islands.

In the hope of affording a remedy to the defective state of the currency of the colonies, it was
determined by the Government in the year 1825,
to introduce British silver coins into all the colonial possessions of the Crown, through the medium
of the Commissariat.

As the measures adopted upon that occasion did
not produce the results expected from them, it is
necessary to inquire into the causes of the failure,
and to notice the errors which appear to have
been at that time committed.

Of those errors, a mistaken estimate of the value
of foreign coins in the money of Great Britain was
the most important.

In forming that estimate, the Mint price of silver

established in the reign of Queen Elizabeth (5s. 2d. per ounce) was referred to, and the fact was over-looked, that since the year 1798, the silver depart-ment of the Mint has been altogether closed against the public; that long before that period, the higher estimate of the value of gold, with respect to silver, at the Mint, than in the market, rendered gold, at the rate of 3l. 17s. 10½d. per ounce, the only measure of property and exchange in this country; and that for more than a century past, neither in our pecuniary contracts at home, nor in our commercial dealings with foreign coun-tries, has the Mint price of 5s. 2d. per ounce for silver been referred to.

To these considerations, the projectors of the measures of 1825, do not appear to have adverted. In estimating the value of foreign coins in sterling money, the ancient standard of the country, accord-ding to which, a pound troy weight of silver was coined into 62 shillings, was alone referred to; and, as it appeared by a table inserted in Dr. Kelly's Universal Cambist, that a Spanish dollar, contained $370\frac{9}{10}$ grains of fine silver, which, at 5s. 2d. per ounce, for standard silver, amount very nearly to 4s. 4d., it was directed that in every colony where the Spanish dollar is a legal tender for the discharge of debt, the British silver money shall also be a legal tender at the rate of 4s. 4d. for the Spanish dollar.

If it had been considered that the value of our

present silver coins has no relation whatever to the ancient Mint price of 5s. 2d. per ounce—that those silver coins are merely tokens or representatives of certain portions of the gold coins, and that by limiting the quantity of them put into circulation, their value is sustained on a level with that of the gold coins, according to the proportionate rates or denominations respectively assigned to each, the gold price of silver only would have been considered in determining the amount of British silver, which, in the colonies, should be deemed a legal tender for a dollar. It would, at the same time, have been seen that the gold price of standard silver was about 5s. per ounce, and that, at that rate, the value of a Spanish dollar in the gold currency of the United Kingdom, and therefore, in British silver, was very nearly 4s. 2d. Being rated in the proclamation of 1825 at 4s. 4d., it was over-valued, with respect to British silver, twopence, or 4 per cent., or which comes to the same thing, British silver was under valued 4 per cent. with respect to the Spanish dollar.

On the introduction of British silver coins into the colonies, instructions were given to the officers of the Commissariat to grant bills upon her Majesty's Treasury, at the rate of 100l. for 103l. (afterwards reduced to 101l. 10s.) of British silver. This measure, it was expected, would secure to the silver the same extrinsic value which it possessed in the mother country, and render it a more useful and convenient instrument of circulation, than the degraded coins, or bits of coins, then circulating in the colonies.

These expectations were not realized. Not only was the concurrent circulation of the Spanish dollar, and British silver, rendered impossible, by the erroneous adaptation to each other of the rates respectively assigned to them, but the free circulation of both was impeded by the high proportionate rate at which the gold coins of Spain were a legal tender.

It has already been observed that the introduction of the gold and silver coins of Spain, and of the Spanish proportions, into the currency of the West Indies, had produced the same consequences there as in Spain; that is, had made gold the predominant metal, and rendered it difficult to retain the silver coins in circulation, at the proportionate rates assigned to them; that at Barbadoes, the current rate of a dollar was 6s. 3d., and of a doubloon 5l. According to these rates, the proportion of fine silver to fine gold was as $16\frac{48}{100}$ to 1, exceeding by more than $4\frac{1}{2}$ per cent. the proportion that prevails in the general market of the commercial world. Similar proportions prevailed in the other British Islands, in the West Indies; and this proportion rendered the concurrent circulation of the dollar and doubloon impracticable.

Now, if the gold doubloon was over-rated more

than $4\frac{1}{2}$ per cent. with reference to the silver dollar, and the dollar was over-rated 4 per cent with reference to sterling money, it follows that the over-valuation of the doubloon, and its divisions, with reference to British silver, was upwards of 8 per cent.

If these considerations had been adverted to in 1825, when it was determined to introduce British silver coins into the colonies, the necessity of determining the rate or value in sterling money, of the gold doubloon, as well as of the silver dollar, would have been apparent.

The error and imperfection of the measure of 1825, then, were two-fold—

1. The over-valuation of the dollar in sterling money.

2. The omission of all notice of the gold coins.

The consequence of that error, and of that omission, will be more distinctly seen when they are considered with reference to the state of the currency of the different colonies; especially those of the West Indies and of America, as it existed at the time when the Royal Proclamation of the 25th March, 1825, was published.

At that time, although the nominal currency of the several islands in the West Indies differed from that of each other, yet in all of them, one doubloon was deemed the equivalent of, and passed current for, sixteen dollars.

At Jamaica for example, the current rate or

denomination of a Spanish dollar had for a long series of years been six shillings and eightpence.

In the year 1773, an Act was passed by the Island Legislature, to give currency to the gold doubloon, at the rate of five pounds, and to certain French and Portuguese coins at proportionate rates; thus making one doubloon equal to fifteen dollars.

A few years afterwards, the Spanish Government ordained by proclamation, that the doubloon should be taken for sixteen dollars; Jamaica followed the example of Spain, and although the local act of 1773, had not been repealed, one doubloon was, conventionally and in practice, deemed the equivalent of sixteen dollars, and passed current, at the rate of five pounds, six shillings and eightpence.

The proportion of fine silver to fine gold, in the money of Jamaica, was thus established as $16\frac{48}{100}$ to 1, or very nearly so.

This over-valuation of the doubloon, or under-valuation of the dollar, rendered it impossible to retain the latter coin in circulation, except, perhaps, in a few small and occasional dealings. In transactions of large amount, dollars computed in the island currency, generally bore a premium, and were imported and exported as merchandize. Gold thus became the standard of exchange in the currency of Jamaica; and the integer, or pound, was three-sixteenths of a doubloon.

Now, as in the currency of Jamaica, "the six-teenth of a doubloon," and " a dollar," were equivalent and convertible expressions, and as the former of the two coins was the cheaper tender of payment, all existing contracts, expressed in terms of that currency, were discharged with doubloons rather than with dollars.

The value of a doubloon in sterling money, reckoning gold of the British standard at $3l.$ $17s.$ $10\frac{1}{2}d.$ per ounce, is sixty-four shillings.

It would have been proper, then, when it was determined to introduce British silver into the currency of those colonies, to have ordained that in every colony where the gold doubloon is a legal tender for the discharge of debts, British silver should also be a legal tender at the rate of sixty-four shillings for the doubloon.

And, in order to give the dollar the chance of circulating concurrently with the doubloon and British silver coin, it would have been proper at the same time, to have ordained that the current rate assigned to the dollar, shall bear the same proportion to the current rate assigned to the six-teenth of a doubloon, as the value of a dollar in sterling money, bears to the value of the sixteenth of a doubloon in sterling money.

The value of a dollar in sterling money, assuming silver of the British standard to be $5s.$ per ounce, is $4s.$ $2\frac{4}{10}d.$, but say $4s.$ $2d.$

Under such a regulation, the rate assigned to

the dollar in the currency of Jamaica, would have been $\dfrac{50d. \times 80d.}{48} = 83\frac{1}{3}d.$, or 6s. $11\frac{1}{3}d.$

But this was not done. The proclamation of the 25th March, 1825, declaring 4s. 4d. in British silver to be the equivalent of a dollar, was issued; and as the value of 4s. 4d. in sterling money is 4 per cent. more than the value of a dollar in sterling money, and more than 8 per cent. above the sterling value of the sixteenth of a doubloon, the concurrent circulation of the doubloon, the dollar, and British silver was rendered impracticable. Gold, at the nominal rate of 5l. 6s. 8d. the doubloon, became practically the basis of the currency of Jamaica; and in order to provide for those small sub-divisions of the currency which are necessary in small payments, and of which gold coins are obviously not susceptible, currency was given, with the acquiescence and consent of the people, but without any legal enactment, to British shillings and sixpences, nominally as the quarters and the eighths of a dollar, but really as the $\frac{1}{64}$th and the $\frac{1}{128}$th of a doubloon.

The concurrent circulation of the doubloon and of British silver coins was thus established; but the silver dollar was excluded from the ordinary channels of circulation, and thus the proclamation of the 25th March, 1825, was rendered nugatory.

At Barbadoes, in like manner, one doubloon was

deemed the equivalent of, and passed current for, sixteen dollars. The current denominations of the two coins were respectively 5*l*. and 6*s*. 3*d*.

In the Report of a Committee of the House of Assembly appointed in the year 1834, to consider the state of the currency, it is mentioned that, at a meeting of the people held seventeen or eighteen years before, it was agreed that the doubloon should be received at the rate of sixteen dollars

The report further states that the dollar, being under-valued as compared with the doubloon, soon ceased to circulate, except in a very limited degree; that, in order to remedy that defect, the British Government, in the year 1822, caused colonial coins to be sent out, consisting of one-fourth, one-eighth, and one-sixteenth of a dollar; that in 1825 an attempt was made to introduce British silver coins into circulation, and a proclamation was issued by the Governor of the Island, fixing such currency value on those coins as made 4*s*. 4*d*. of British silver equivalent to a Spanish dollar; that a few half-crowns were introduced, but very soon disappeared.

In proceeding to the consideration of the currency rates at which British silver coins should be introduced into the Island, the Committee observed that the value of the doubloon having been fixed at 5*l*. currency, to reduce that value would be to interfere with all contracts which had taken place during the period above mentioned : it would increase the difficulties of debtors, and would be an act of gross injustice. The Committee was, therefore, of opinion, that the value of the doubloon, at the currency rate, should be taken as the standard, and upon this principle they proceeded to fix a current value on the British coins. They found, on inquiry, that the average price of a doubloon, in London, was about 3*l.* 4*s.* sterling, and the currency rate being 5*l.*, they concluded that the currency value of the sovereign should be 1*l.* 11*s.* 3*d.*, and that the English silver coins should be rated in proportion to the value of the sovereign.

A Bill, in conformity with the recommendation of the Committee, was brought into the House of Assembly, but not being approved by the Governor, it did not pass into a law.

In the early part of 1836, the distress for small change became so great that the Governor, Sir Lionel Smith, was induced to issue a proclamation, fixing the current value of the English shilling at 1*s.* 6*d.*, which, as the currency rate of the dollar was 6*s.* 3*d.*, made 4*s.* 2*d.* of English money equal to a dollar.

This proclamation was limited to a period of six months.

Previous to its renewal a meeting of the principal planters and merchants was held at Bridgetown, at which meeting resolutions were passed, declaring that great and general embarrassment was experienced in all the money transactions of the community, in consequence of the expiration of the term limited by the proclamation sanctioning the circulation of British silver coin, at a fixed rate; that the evils consequent on the want of a circulating medium of silver, in small denominations of coin, fell chiefly on the planters and apprenticed labourers, the loss to the latter being great, as they were thus prevented, to a considerable extent, from obtaining employment during their extra hours and on free days; and that it was expedient to present a petition to the Governor, requesting him to take the matter into his serious consideration.

The proclamation was subsequently renewed, with the approbation of the Lords of the Treasury and the Secretary of State.

The dollar and British silver were thus placed on a just level with each other, but both being undervalued with reference to the current rate of the doubloon, neither the one nor the other could be retained in circulation ; and the want of small silver coins, for change, continued as perplexing as before.

In all the other Islands of the West Indies difficulties were felt similar to those experienced at Jamaica and Barbadoes. In all of them, one doubloon was deemed equal to sixteen dollars. In all, the over-valuation of the doubloon precluded the concurrent circulation of the silver dollar.

It thus appears that the proclamation of the 25th of March, 1825, with respect to the currency of the colonies, was nugatory and inoperative, and that in the West Indies British silver coins obtained circulation only in consequence of the British shilling being paid and received, with the consent of the people, and without the authority of law, as the quarter of a gold dollar, that is to say, as the quarter of one-sixteenth of a doubloon.

In 1835 the army rate of the doubloon was reduced from 69s. 4d. to 66s.

The grounds of that reduction are stated in a Minute of the Treasury Board, dated June 19, 1835; from which Minute the following is an extract:—

" In fixing an army rate on foreign gold coins, " my Lords consider it to be a desirable object to " render it, if possible, indifferent to the soldier " whether he receives his pay in those coins, or in " foreign silver money; and as the doubloon is " intrinsically equivalent to about $15\frac{5}{21}$ dollars, " and, in paying the army on foreign stations, the " dollar is valued at 4s. 4d., the corresponding value " of the gold piece may, with sufficient accuracy, " be considered to be 66s. Accordingly, their " Lordships are pleased to direct, that so long as it " shall be considered expedient to continue the army " rate fixed on the Spanish dollar in the year 1825, " the doubloon shall be issued to the troops at the " rate of sixty-six shillings, and the several divisions " of that coin at proportional rates."

The loss sustained by the troops in the West Indies, when paid in doubloons, was thus reduced from upwards of 8 per cent. to about $3\frac{1}{2}$ per cent. When paid in dollars, however, they continued subject to the same loss as before. The object aimed at in the new regulation, namely, that of rendering it a matter of indifference to the soldier whether he received his pay in foreign gold or in foreign silver money, was not attained. The troops were certainly benefitted by the alteration, that is, they were less injured when paid in doubloons than when paid in dollars; but the main causes of grievance were not removed by it.

THE REMEDIAL MEASURES ADOPTED IN THE YEAR 1838.

In this unsatisfactory and conflicting state, the currency of the British Islands, in the West Indies, continued until the year 1838, when the subject was again taken into consideration by the Treasury Board.

After much investigation and inquiry, it was determined to revoke the Order in Council of the 25th March, 1825, so far as respected Her Majesty's colonies and plantations in America and the West Indies; and to issue a proclamation for declaring and ordaining, that throughout the West India Colonies, including the province of British Guiana, the doubloon shall circulate, and be received in payment, as being of the full value of sixty-four shillings sterling, current money of the United Kingdom; and that the dollar shall circulate, and be received in payment, as being of the full value of four shillings and two pence, like current money of the United Kingdom. And in all payments to be made in any of the said colonies, tender of payment in doubloons and dollars, or either of them, at the rate aforesaid, shall be deemed and taken to be a lawful tender, in the same manner as if such tender had been made in the current coin of the United Kingdom.

Immediately after the publication of the above-mentioned Order in Council and Proclamation, instructions were transmitted by the Secretary of State to the governors of the several colonies in the West Indies, directing them to issue proclamations for the purpose of declaring the nominal rate and value of the doubloon, the dollar, and the British shilling, expressed in terms of the currency of those several colonies, according to the proportions and relative value of those coins fixed in Her Majesty's Proclamation.

In the instructions from the Secretary of State upon that occasion, it was observed that, as all contracts in the West Indian islands have reference to the over-valued gold coins, it had been deemed proper to retain the present denomination of the doubloon, and to raise the present denomination of the dollar in the proportion of $\frac{64 \times 12}{50} = 15\cdot 36$ to 16; that the effect of this alteration would be to give to $15\cdot 36$ dollars the same current denomination as was then given to one doubloon, and to render $15\cdot 36$ dollars and one doubloon equivalent tenders of payment for the same amount of nominal currency.

In pursuance of those instructions, proclamations were issued in the several islands of the West Indies, declaring the currency rates at which the doubloon, the dollar, and British silver coins shall circulate and be deemed a legal tender.

Those rates are exhibited in the following tabular statement:—

	Doubloon.	British Shilling.	Dollar.
	£. s. d.	s. d.	s. d.
Jamaica . . .	5 6 8	1 8	6 11$\frac{1}{3}$
Barbadoes . . .	5 0 0	1 6$\frac{3}{4}$	6 6
Trinidad . . . Grenada . . . St. Vincent . . Dominica . . .	8 0 0	2 6	10 5
Antigua . . . St. Kitts . . . Montserrat . . Nevis	7 4 0	2 3	9 4$\frac{1}{2}$

It will be seen by the foregoing statement, that, in the adaptation of the nominal currencies of the several islands in the West Indies, to the doubloon, the dollar, and British silver coins, according to the proportions fixed in Her Majesty's proclamation of the 14th September, 1838, the introduction of inconvenient fractions was unavoidable. At Jamaica, for instance, the rate assigned to the dollar was 6s. 11$\frac{1}{3}$d., which rate prevented, in a considerable degree, the easy circulation and payment of that coin in single pieces.

Another circumstance of a like nature prevented the free circulation of British silver coins.

In all the West Indian colonies the peasantry and labouring population are in the habit of computing their money dealings in " bitts," of which " bitts" the number reckoned equal to a dollar is different at different places. Thus, a dollar is reckoned at—

		Bitts.
Barbadoes, as	.	10
Trinidad	.	9
Demerara	.	12
Antigua ⎫		
St. Kitts ⎪		
Nevis ⎬	.	12
Montserrat ⎪		
Dominica ⎭		

Now as British silver coins cannot be accurately adjusted to those divisions, without inconvenient fractions, they are, in some of the islands, under-valued by this class of the community, with reference to the dollar; and when occasionally introduced into circulation, are picked up by speculators and others who are able, in larger quantities, to obtain for them their just value

It is certainly desirable when a change is made in the currency of any country to consult, as much as possible, the accustomed habits, and even the prejudices of the people, when that can be done without the neglect or violation of any important principle. It should be borne in mind, however, that the chief object of the measures adopted in 1838, namely, the correct adjustment to each other of the several coins in circulation in the colonies, according to their respective values, and the making plain the way for the future conversion of the various monies of account into sterling denominations, without interfering with existing contracts, and the obligations and rights of debtors and creditors, could not have been attained without some inconvenience of this nature.

At Jamaica, the above-mentioned difficulty was removed, and the ultimate object of the measure of 1838 finally accomplished, by an Act passed by the legislature of the Island, at the close of the following year (3 Vict c. 39), for making the currency of the United Kingdom of Great Britain and Ireland the currency of Jamaica, and for declaring all receipts and payments as therein set forth, to be had, made, or done, according to such currency of the United Kingdom.

By this Act it is ordained that all gifts, contracts, bargains, sales, and all debts due or to become due, which shall have been or shall be acknowledged at any time before the commencement of the Act, according or with reference to the currency of Jamaica, shall be construed and carried into effect, and shall be discharged and satisfied as follows : that is to say, that every sum of the currency of the Island then due, or thereafter to become due, or to be accounted for, shall be equivalent to, stated as, and be liable to be paid at the rate of 100*l.* of the currency of the United Kingdom, for every 166*l.* 13*s.* 4*d.* of the present currency of Jamaica, in the several coins declared by the Act to be legal tender.

It is, then, ordained that from and after the commencement of the Act, the doubloon shall be a legal tender, at and after the rate of 64s., the dollar at 4s. 2d.; and that the gold and silver coins of Great Britain shall be a legal tender to any amount at the rates current in Great Britain.

This change in the denominations of the currency of Jamaica does not appear to have been attended with the smallest difficulty or inconvenience. The Queen's proclamation of the 13th September, 1838, had cleared the way for it. Existing money contracts and engagements were not in the slightest degree interfered with. A debt of a given amount, whether expressed in terms of the previous currency or of the new denominations, could be legally discharged with the same number of doubloons, dollars, or British gold and silver coins, as before. And with respect to debts and engagements subsequently incurred, as the relation between the old and the new money of account was sufficiently obvious, and as the one is readily convertible into the other by an easy arithmetical process, no misapprehension or mistake was at all likely to arise. Nor has any difficulty or inconvenience been experienced by the peasantry and labouring population in the application of the rule. This class of the community has abandoned in a great degree, if not altogether, the use of the terms " bitts," and " dogs," and has adapted the British denominations of money, of which they now correctly understand the nature and the import.

The conversion of the former currency of Jamaica into the sterling money of Great Britain is effected by deducting 40 per cent. from the amount of that currency. Thus $\dfrac{100 \times 100}{166\frac{2}{3}} = 40$; or, which comes to the same thing, the current rate of a doubloon having been 5*l*. 6*s*. 8*d*., a deduction of 40 per cent. from that rate leaves 64*s*. as the sterling value of a doubloon.

In the local Act above referred to, it is accordingly directed that 100*l*. of the currency of the United Kingdom shall be deemed equal to 166*l*. 13*s*. 4*d*. of the currency of Jamaica.

In many of the other British islands of the West Indies, their old forms and denominations of money are still retained. It may, however, be expected that in no long time they will all follow the example of Jamaica, abolish their objectionable money denominations, adopt the British or sterling money of account, and thus get rid of the inconveniences and anomalies which are now experienced.

Previously to the year 1839, the currency of British Guiana differed materially and essentially from that of the West Indian islands; and as the peculiar state of that currency involved considerations of considerable importance, it may be useful briefly to describe it.

In that province accounts were kept in guilders, stivers, and pennings.

1 guilder = 20 stivers
1 stiver = 16 pennings.

The metallic money of the province consisted of

1. Tokens coined at the British Mint, of various denominations, from three guilders downwards.

2. British silver coins.

3. Mexican and South American dollars.

A three-guilder piece contained 294 grains of fine silver, and was worth, in sterling money, very nearly 3s. 4d.

Neither doubloons nor dollars were legally current in the colony at fixed rates; but in the ordinary interchange of the province three guilders were deemed equal to one dollar.

The only coins which were legally current were three-guilder tokens, and their sub-divisions, and British silver, at the rate of 14 guilders for twenty shillings; and as a dollar passed for 3 guilders, its value was reckoned equal to 4*s*. 3¾*d*. in sterling money.

Besides the guilder tokens and their sub-divisions, a large amount of inconvertible paper money, issued by the local Government, and consisting of joe and half-joe notes (the joe being deemed equal to 22 guilders), was in circulation in the colony, and deemed a legal tender of payment.

As the quantity of those guilder pieces could not be increased without an additional coinage of them at the Royal Mint, consequently without the express permission and authority of the Home Government, and as the paper was not convertible into specie, the value of the currency was liable to considerable variations, which were indicated by the varying state of the foreign exchanges.

When the exchange with England was 14 guilders 8 stivers for one pound sterling,—then, as 14 guilders 8 stivers were deemed in the colony to be equal to $4\frac{8}{10}$ dollars, and as the value of $4\frac{8}{10}$ dollars, in London, was 20*s*. sterling, the exchange with England, and the currency value of a Mexican dollar, were exactly at par.

The ultimate metallic check to a fall in the value of the Guiana currency, with reference to the money of other countries, were the silver tokens.

The sterling value of a three-guilder piece being 3*s*. 4*d*., the value of 20*s*. in sterling money was equal to that of 18 guilders. Hence it happened that the exchange with England fluctuated between the extremes above mentioned, namely, 14 guilders 8 stivers per pound sterling, and 18 guilders per pound sterling.

When 18 guilders were given for a bill of exchange on England, for one pound, the currency was depreciated 20 per cent. below the dollar standard.

The exchange occasionally fell below this point, and it became profitable to export the silver tokens. This diminution of the metallic part of the currency, and the limitation of the amount of the paper currency—or perhaps a simultaneous contraction of it—increased the value of the currency, and raised the exchange with England to 14 guilders per pound sterling.

This state of the currency of Guiana exemplifies, in a remarkable manner, the principle and the effect of *limitation*. By limiting the amount of the Government paper, its value was occasionally 20 per cent. above the value of the metallic money with which it was interchanged. By a further contraction, its value might have been raised still higher, and dollars have been forced into the colony from abroad.

Soon after the receipt of Her Majesty's Order in Council of the 13th September, 1838, the Governor of British Guiana issued a proclamation, declaring that from and after the 15th November, 1838, the dollar, the doubloon, and the silver coins of the United Kingdom, shall be received and taken at the following rates, that is to say,— the doubloon at the rate of 46 guilders 1⅗ stivers, and its fractional parts in like proportion ; the dollar at the rate of 3 guilders, and its fractional parts in like proportion ; the British shilling at 14⅞ stivers, and all other British silver coins, and the fractional parts of the British shilling, in the like proportion.

On the 29th January, 1839, another proclamation was issued for establishing dollars and cents of a dollar, as the denominations of monies of account in British Guiana, instead of guilders, stivers, and pennings.

By this ordinance it is enacted, that " all ex-
" isting accounts, notes of hand, or other claims
" of whatsoever nature, payable or receivable in
" guilders, shall be payable or recoverable in dol-
" lars currency, the amount in guilders being first
" brought into dollars currency, at the rate and in
" the proportion of three guilders to one dollar
" currency; and that all coins which by law have
" been declared to be legal tenders for debts con-
" tracted in guilders, as also the colonial paper
" currency of Demerara and Essequibo, commonly
" called joe notes, of whatever amount the same.
" may be, and half-joe notes, so long as the ordi-
" nances or proclamations by which the said paper
" currency has been made a legal tender shall re-
" main in force, shall be a legal tender for the

" same said accounts, notes of hand, and other
" claims, when brought into dollars currency, at
" the rate and in the proportion aforesaid."

This change in the money of account in Guiana,
from guilders, stivers, and pennings, to dollars and
cents, and the rendering the paper money of the
local Government convertible into specie at the
will of the holder, it was expected, would not only
promote the free circulation of British silver coins
in the colony, but likewise facilitate the transition
to the sterling money of account, if, at a future
period, it should be deemed desirable and expedient
to make such a further change.

A difficulty, however, existed, which required
to be removed before the benefits which it was
expected would result from the above-cited ordinance, could be fully realized. That difficulty
consisted in fixing the relative value of the dollar
and British silver coins, in those denominations to
which the negroes and the lower classes of the
community had long been accustomed. The fractional parts of the currency, as universally understood by those classes, are denominated " bitts,"—
4 bitts to the guilder, 12 bitts to the dollar. Now the
British shilling (reckoning the dollar at 4s. 2d.) is
not susceptible of a corresponding division, without
an inconvenient fraction, which fraction the labouring population could not understand, or with which
they were averse from being troubled. Hence it
was, that when the British shilling was legally

current in the colony, at the rate of 14 stivers, and the sixpence at 7 stivers, the lower classes, finding that they could not pass the shilling for 15 stivers, or a quarter of a dollar, would receive it for only $2\frac{1}{2}$ bitts, or $12\frac{1}{2}$ stivers, and the sixpence for only one bitt, or 5 stivers.

A similar difficulty existed with regard to the adaptation of the bitt to the new denominations of dollars and cents. As a shilling is legally current under the ordinance of the 29th January, 1839, for only 24 cents, or 4 per cent. less than a quarter of a dollar, the peasantry and labouring population would take it for only $2\frac{1}{2}$ bitts, and the sixpence for 1 bitt.

This difficulty was afterwards overcome by an ordinance of the local Government, declaring the dollar to be divisible into $12\frac{1}{2}$ bitts, thus making a shilling equal to 3 bitts, a fourpenny-piece to 1 bitt, and a twopenny-piece to a half bitt.

It remains to notice an objection which may perhaps be made to the principle involved in the Queen's proclamation of the 13th September, 1838. It may be said that that proclamation was an attempt to establish a double standard of gold and silver—to fix the relative value of the two metals in the coins, although their value relatively to each other in the market is continually varying; that if the value of silver, with respect to gold, should permanently fall, the doubloon, and British gold and silver, could not be maintained in concurrent circulation with the dollar of 4s. 2d.; and that if, on the other hand, the value of gold, relatively to silver, should materially fall, the silver dollar would be driven from circulation, and thus the evils, which it was the object of the proclamation of 1838 to remedy, would be again experienced.

This objection must, to some extent, be admitted. It must be allowed that if the market value of gold and silver should permanently vary from the proportion fixed in the Order in Council and proclamation of 1838, the cheaper metal will practically become the principal measure of value and exchange in the colonies, and that all money contracts will be discharged in that cheaper metal.

It should, however, be observed, that although during the last forty years the value of the two metals, relatively to each other, in the market, has undergone frequent fluctuations (the value of silver relatively to gold, alternately falling and rising, and rising and falling), yet their *average* relative value has continued nearly constant ; and that when the Order in Council and proclamation of September, 1838, were issued, there existed no great reason to apprehend that it would not continue so.

It should further be observed, that if in the year 1838, it had been determined to make one of the metals only the principal measure of property and exchange in the West Indies and British

America, it would have been necessary to have
excluded from the circulation, either the doubloon,
and the gold and silver money of the mother
country, or the silver dollar of Mexico and South
America.

Suppose it had been determined to make the
silver dollar and its divisions, the sole legal tender
of payment, and to leave the doubloon and all
other gold coins to find their value in the market,
that is, to be purchased and sold at varying prices,
as against silver dollars—it would have been necessary, in that case, to have fixed a higher proportionate rate (proportionate with reference to the
relative value of gold and silver in the market), to
the dollar than had previously been assigned to
the doubloon.

At Jamaica, for example, where the same rate
was given to a dollar as to one-sixteenth of a doubloon, namely 6s. 8d., it would have been necessary
to have raised the denomination of the silver dollar
to 7s. 1d.,* in order to render that coin a cheaper
tender of payment than the doubloon; for although
in the case supposed, no legal rate would have
been assigned to the doubloon, yet if the dollar
had continued to be a legal tender at its former

---

* This rate assigned to the dollar, compared with the doubloon at
5l. 6s. 8d., would make fine silver to fine gold, as 15¼ to 1 ; and as the
relative value of the two metals, in the general market, is about 15¾ to
1, the assignment of the rate of 7s. 1d. to the dollar would have rendered that coin a cheaper tender of payment than the doubloon at
5l. 6s. 8d., by about 1½ per cent.

rate, namely 6s. 8d., the doubloon would have continued *in practice* to be received at the rate of 5l. 6s. 8d., and would have ousted the dollar.

The only means, then, of establishing the dollar as the sole legal tender of payment, in the West India Islands, would have been to give to that coin a much higher rate, in terms of the currency of those islands, than had previously been assigned to one-sixteenth of a doubloon.

But to have done this would have been to do violence to, and unsettle, all existing money contracts and engagements. The man who had bound himself to pay 53l. 6s. 8d. in Jamaica currency, and who could have discharged his obligation only by the payment of 10 doubloons or 160 dollars, would now be enabled to pay his debt with $150\frac{5}{7}$ dollars, which in the general market of the world are worth only 9·85 doubloons. The creditor would thus receive $1\frac{1}{2}$ per cent. less than the value of the doubloons to which, if he had been paid in that coin, he would have been justly entitled.

Besides this consideration, it should be borne in mind, that if the Spanish dollar and other silver coins had been made the principal measure of property and exchange in the West Indies, the establishment of the sterling money of account, and the introduction of the gold and silver coins of the mother country, would have been rendered wholly impracticable.

Although it appears sufficiently clear that, in

the year 1838, it would have been impossible to have established silver as the basis of the currency of the West Indies, without disturbing existing contracts, yet as a contrary opinion was at that time entertained by many persons whose knowledge and experience gave them a fair title to the most respectful attention, and as a like opinion still occasionally prevails, it may not be useless to enter into some further examination of this point.

It was contended that the foundation of existing contracts in the West Indies, was not a gold, but a silver standard of money.

Let this proposition be tried on a simple case.

A debtor owed 160*l.* currency in Jamaica, or 150*l.* currency in Barbadoes, or 240*l.* currency in Trinidad. At all those places, the only means by which the debtor could discharge his obligations was by the payment, or the tender of payment, of 30 doubloons, or 480 dollars. The debtor knew, when he entered into the contract, that he could legally discharge his obligation either with gold or with silver. The creditor knew that the debt due to him might, and most probably would, be paid in the cheapest legal tender. As 480 dollars are worth more, in the general market of the world, than 30 doubloons, the cheapest tender of payment, according to the monetary laws and regulations of the West Indies, as they existed in 1838, was gold. Both parties, then, contemplated a payment in gold. To have denied this, would have been to deny that, in the West Indies, one doubloon was deemed equal to sixteen dollars. To have admitted this fact, would have been to admit that the foundation of the contract of debt was a gold standard of money.

The point in question may be further illustrated by adverting to what happens in France. A debtor in France owes 1000 francs; he can legally discharge the debt either with 50 twenty-franc pieces in gold, or with 1000 francs in silver. According to the monetary laws and regulations of France, silver is the cheapest legal tender; he therefore pays the debt in silver. In entering into the contract of debt, a payment in silver was contemplated by both debtor and creditor. In France, then, silver is the basis and foundation of existing contracts.

In like manner, and upon the same principle, previously to the year 1838, the basis and foundation of contracts in the West Indies was not a silver, but a gold standard of money.

CURRENCY OF THE BRITISH PROVINCES OF NORTH AMERICA.

The rate or value assigned to certain foreign coins in most of the colonial possessions of the Crown, appears to have been originally determined by the people, and afterwards altered and modified by Acts passed by the local legislatures, and assented to by the Crown.

This was especially the case in the West Indies and North America.

In the British provinces of North America, although accounts were kept, and bargains made, in the terms of pounds, shillings, and pence, the Spanish dollar was considered as the principal measure of exchange, and the basis of pecuniary contracts.. The nominal rate assigned to the dollar was four shillings and sixpence. This rate corresponds with the value of that coin in sterling money, as stated in a table of assays, weights, and values, made by Sir Isaac Newton, at the Royal Mint, by order of the Privy Council, in the year 1717; in which table it is stated, that the piastre of Spain, or Seville piece of 8 rialls, weighed 17 dwts. 12 grains, equal to 17 dwts. 10 grains of silver of the British standard, and that its value was four shillings and sixpence in English money.

Notwithstanding that, a dollar of the present coinage contains 14 grains of fine silver less than the piastre of 1717, and that the standard of money in Great Britain has been changed from silver to gold, the valuation of the dollar at four shillings and sixpence is still adhered to, in computations of exchange between the United States of America and Great Britain, affording a remarkable example of the tenacity with which long-established habits are retained by the people in matters which involve, or are supposed to involve, their pecuniary interests.

From causes, of which it would now be difficult to ascertain the origin, the nominal value of the dollar has undergone a considerable change, both in the United States of America and in the British American provinces. In New England, it is now six shillings; in New York, eight shillings; in Pennsylvania, seven shillings and sixpence; and in Nova Scotia, five shillings.

Throughout the British provinces of North America, the Halifax denomination of five shillings has long been the prevailing one; and the nominal par of exchange with England was computed by adding one-ninth to the old valuation of the dollar at four shillings and sixpence; or, which is the same thing, $111\frac{1}{9}l.$ Halifax currency, are considered to be the par of exchange for $100l.$ sterling.

But as in consequence of the diminished quantity of fine silver contained in the dollar now in circulation, compared with the quantity of fine silver contained in the Spanish dollar coined previously to the year 1728, and the alteration which has been made in the metallic standard of the mother country, the sterling value of a dollar is now only four shillings and two-pence, the real par of exchange (disregarding, at present, any slight variation which may occasionally take place in the value of gold and silver relatively to each other) is 120*l.*, Halifax currency, or 480 dollars for 100*l.* sterling.

Although the Spanish dollar has always been considered as the principal measure of property and exchange in the British provinces of America, yet as other foreign coins of gold and silver were declared by Acts of the local legislatures to be a legal tender of payment, at certain nominal rates, and as those rates were not the same in all the provinces, it is desirable shortly to trace the history of the currency of each of the British American provinces, up to the period when Her Majesty's proclamation of the 13th September, 1838, was promulgated.

Lower Canada.

In this province, it was enacted by the local Act of 48 Geo. III., c. 8, that the British

guinea weighing 5 dwts. 6 grains shall pass for
1*l*. 3*s*. 4*d*.

	£.	s.	d.
Johannes of Portugal, weighing 18 dwts. . .	4	0	0
Moidore of ditto, 6 dwts. 18 grs.	1	10	0
Milled doubloon, 17 dwts.	3	14	6
French Louis d'or, 5 dwts. 4 grs.	1	2	8
American eagle, 11 dwts. 6 grs.*	2	10	0

SILVER COINS.

	£.	s.	d.
British crown	0	5	6
,, shilling	0	1	1
Spanish milled dollar	0	5	0
,, pestareen	0	1	0
French crown	0	5	6
,, piece of 4 livres 10 sols . . .	0	4	2
,, ,, 36 sols	0	1	8
,, ,, 24 sols	0	1	1
American dollar	0	5	0

By the 2nd section of the Act, it was ordained
that for every grain the British, Portugal, or
American gold coins shall weigh more than the
weights specified above; when weighed singly,
2¾*d*. shall be added, and, when less, 2¼*d*. shall be
deducted from the values above stated; and 2⅓*d*.
be added to, or deducted from, the Spanish and
French coins.

Section 7 enacts that, in payments above 20*l*.,
gold coins shall be weighed, in bulk, at the option
of either party; those of Great Britain, Portugal,
and America, together, at 89*s*. per ounce, troy

---

* The eagle, at that time, contained 247½ grains of fine gold, and
was better by 6·68 per cent. than the eagle of 1834, which contains
only 232 grains of fine gold.

weight, and those of Spain and France at 87s. 8d. per ounce, troy ; a deduction of half a grain being made as a compensation for loss on paying away the pieces singly.

By the 10 and 11 Geo. IV., the rate assigned to pestareens was reduced from 1s. to 10d.

The coin to which the highest relative value was given by this Act, was the French crown, which, when of full weight, should contain 403 grains of fine silver, and with reference to the dollar of the United States, is worth, in Halifax currency, 5s. $5\frac{14}{100}d$. Being rated at 5s. 6d., French crowns were over-valued in that relation $1\frac{3}{10}$ per cent.

As, however, the quantity of French crowns and half-crowns in the province was comparatively small, their value would probably have been sustained on a level with that of the American dollar, had it not been for the depressing influence of the paper money in circulation.

When the foreign exchange was adverse, and a demand arose for metallic money for exportation, the issuers of paper money were enabled to shield themselves from, at least to mitigate the effect of, a demand upon them for coin, by paying their outstanding notes with French half-crowns, which, being greatly injured by wear, were of much less value abroad than in the province, and were not therefore exported.

The dollars of Mexico and South America are

better by about the half of one per cent. than the dollars of the United States; and as in the Act above-mentioned, they were both rated at five shillings currency, the latter must be considered as the standard to which all money contracts had reference.

The Order in Council of the 25th March, 1825, by which four British shillings and four-pence were declared to be the equivalent of a Spanish dollar, was inoperative in this province, as it was in all the colonies, for reasons which have already been explained. The same cause excluded English copper money, and occasioned the introduction into the province of a debased and spurious copper coinage.

Upper Canada.

Before the year 1827, the same rates were assigned to British and foreign coins in this province as in Lower Canada.

In that year, an Act was passed (7 Geo. IV. c. 4), by which it was enacted, that the Spanish milled dollar, and the American dollar, shall pass current, and be a legal tender, at the rate of 5s.; the British crown, at the rate of 5s. 9d.; the British shilling, at the rate of 1s. 2d; and all the higher and lower denominations of British silver coins at proportionate rates; and that British copper money shall pass current, and be a legal tender, at the rate of ten-pence for one shilling currency, in payments not exceeding one shilling current money of the province.

This Act appears to have been suggested by, and founded on, the royal proclamation of the 13th March, 1825, by which four shillings and four-pence were declared to be the equivalent of a Spanish dollar. As, by this Act, British silver coins were under-rated, with reference to the real value of the dollar, they were driven from the circulation of the province.

In the year 1836, an Act was passed by the legislature of this province, by which Act the current rate of an English crown was raised from 5s. 9d. to 6s., and that of an English shilling from 1s. 2d. to 1s. 3d.

By this Act the British sovereign, which had not before been specifically rated in any Act of the local legislature, was made a legal tender at the rate of 1l. 4s. 4d. of current money, and the American eagle at the rate of 2l. 10s. current money.* The rate of the dollar, and that of all other coins, were allowed to remain un-altered.

By the new rates a dollar was made equal to 4s. 2d. sterling, in English crowns, and to 4s. sterling in English shillings.

The framers of this Act do not appear to have considered that the regulations which it ordains

* See note, page 66.

would necessarily drive dollars, crowns, and half-crowns from circulation, and that British shillings and sixpences only would remain; for the shilling, instead of being rated in exact proportion to the dollar and the crown, that is to say, at 1s. 2⅖d., was rated at 1s. 3d. This was probably done in order to avoid the inconvenience of small fractions. But the small fraction, in this case, was a matter of essential importance. The shilling being rated at 1s. 3d. currency, and the dollar at 5s. currency, made the dollar equal to four British shillings, being an over-valuation of the shilling, with reference to the dollar, of exactly 4 per cent.

To this extent, the Act affected all money contracts existing in the province at the time of its being passed.

There was another discrepancy in this Act, which it is important to notice. The gold sovereign was made a legal tender for 1l. 4s. 4d., while at the same time twenty British shillings were to pass for 1l. 5s. currency.

This discrepancy probably originated in the wish to establish, in Upper Canada, the same proportion of fine silver to fine gold that obtained in the monetary regulations of the United States. In the United States, an eagle containing 232½ grains of fine gold is a legal tender for 10 dollars, containing 3712·5 grains of fine silver—making the value of silver to gold in the proportion of 16 to 1, —which exceeds the proportion that obtains in the general market of the commercial world by nearly one and a half per cent.

The effect of this Act is shown in the following statement:—

A debt of 100*l.* currency might be discharged with 1,600 British shillings, of which the sterling value is 80*l.*; or with 333⅓ crowns, of which the sterling value is 83*l.* 6*s.* 8*d.*; or with 82¼⁴⁄₃ sovereigns, of which the sterling value is 82*l.* 2*s.* 6*d.*; or with 40 eagles, of which the sterling value is 82*l.* 2*s.* 6*d.*; or with 400 dollars, of which the sterling value is 83*l.* 6*s.* 8*d.*

It thus appears that, under this Act, the cheapest tender of payment (French crowns and half-crowns having been excluded from the circulation by the 11 George IV., c. 6) were British shillings and sixpences; and as a debtor will always avail himself of the cheapest tender of payment, English crowns and half-crowns, dollars, sovereigns, and eagles were practically excluded from circulation. The integer or pound currency, in Upper Canada, was 16 British shillings; and assuming a Mexican dollar, containing 373 grains of fine silver, to be worth 4*s.* 2*d.* in English money, and the dollar of the United States (371¼ grains of silver) to be worth 4*s.* 1¾*d.* in English money, the former was under-valued, in reference to British silver coins, 4 per cent., and the latter 3½ per cent.

From the foregoing statements it appears that, previously to the year 1838, the basis of the currency of Lower Canada was silver; that in Upper Canada the cheapest tender of payment were British shillings and sixpences; and that from both provinces, gold coins, in consequence of being rated too low with reference to foreign silver coins in the one—and with reference to British shillings in the other,—were excluded.

The inconveniences chiefly complained of, with respect to the metallic money of Lower Canada, were the deteriorated condition and limited supply of French crowns and half-crowns, and the degraded state of the copper money.

With a view to remedy these defects, and to prevent the frequent necessity of importing from the United States large sums, in specie, at a considerable expence to the provincial banks, it was proposed, on behalf of those banks, that an application should be made to the Home Government, for the fabrication of silver coins at the British Mint, for the special use of the colony; and that, in order to prevent all inducement to export them, they should be made a legal tender at a higher rate than would correspond with their value as bullion.

As this proposal was strenuously urged by its advocates, and as similar proposals have frequently been made from other colonies, it may be well in this place to show that the proposal, if adopted, would have afforded only a temporary relief, and that every scheme of this nature must ultimately fail of accomplishing the object aimed at.

The proposal proceeded on the supposition that the coins which it was suggested should be coined and issued, would possess, in the colony, an extrinsic value as coin, over and above their value as bullion, and that they would constantly preserve that extrinsic value.

It is necessary to examine this supposition.

Suppose the proposed pieces were declared to be a legal tender of payment, at the rates which are given to the dollar and its divisions, the question then is—whether, being of less intrinsic value than the dollar, the value of the new pieces could be sustained on a level with that coin.

Now it may safely be concluded that if, at any time, the amount of the new coins put into circulation were to exceed the amount of dollars, which could, at that time, be absorbed and employed in the business of domestic interchange and traffic, the superiority of their value as coin, over their value as bullion, would be extinguished —even although no paper money were in circulation to affect that value.

We have to enquire, then, whether the quantity put into circulation could be duly and properly restrained and limited.

This would, in a great degree, if not altogether, depend on the principle and the mode of their original issue.

There are two ways, in either of which such coins might be issued. 1st. They might be coined at the Mint on account of the Government, and issued in the colony, through the medium of the Commissariat, or in Government disbursements. 2nd. The Mint might be opened to the public for the coinage of silver into the required pieces, at a certain fixed rate of seignorage, or Mint charge.

In the first case, the new pieces would be issued to the troops stationed in the province, or in payment for supplies, at the same nominal rate as is given to the dollar, and its divisions; but as there would exist no natural or necessary check to the issue, that issue might be carried to such an extent as to bring down the value of the new coins, as compared with the dollar, to the level of their intrinsic value, and thus not only injuriously affect existing contracts, but introduce uncertainty and confusion into all future pecuniary dealings.

With respect to the second case, that of opening the British Mint to the public for the coinage of the proposed coins, at a fixed rate of seignorage, or Mint charge, it must be admitted that when the State charges a seignorage for coinage, the coined pieces will generally exceed the value of the metal of which they are made, by the amount of the seignorage. Only so long as they do so, will that metal be brought by the public to the Mint for coinage. When an excessive quantity is thrown into circulation, and the market price of silver rises above the Mint price, all applications to the Mint for coinage naturally ceases, until the excess is absorbed, or until a fall in the market price of silver encourages further coinage.

There is thus a correcting principle in constant operation; and if there were no issues of paper money, the extrinsic value created by a seignorage might very possibly be preserved.

But in Canada, as in nearly all the British colonies, there is a circulation of paper money on an extensive scale ; the enlargement and contraction of which depend altogether on the judgment and, discretion of the banks that issue it.

Now, as the currency of a country may as effectually be increased with paper as with coin, it is impossible, when banks are established with an unlimited power of issue, to prevent such an enlargement of the whole currency—paper and coin —as will keep down the value of the whole to the level of the intrinsic value of the coin in which the paper is redeemable. To that level it must fall before the check arising from the obligation which the banks are under, of paying their notes in specie on demand, begins to operate. " If," says Mr. Ricardo, " the seignorage of gold coin were 5 per " cent, the currency by an abundant issue of bank " notes, might be really depreciated 5 per cent. " before it would be the interest of the holders to " demand coin for the purpose of melting it into " bullion."

The introduction of coins which have borne a high seignorage, would then have enabled the banks of Canada, without the risk of being exposed to a demand for specie for exportation, to have enlarged their promissory circulation to such an extent, as would have reduced the value of the currency to a level with the *intrinsic* value of the coins; and have produced a corresponding depression in the exchange with England and the United States.

During the progress of the depreciation, the banks would indeed have derived from it considerable advantage at the expense of their creditors. But that advantage could have been only temporary. As soon as the change in the value of the currency had been completely established, the same complaints of a scarcity of silver would have been made, and the same difficulties have been experienced as before.

The suggestions of the Canadian banks were not adopted by the Home Government. All applications of a like nature from other colonies have likewise very properly been refused.

It has already been stated that on the promulgation of her Majesty's proclamation of the 13th September, 1838, fixing the rates of the doubloon and the dollar at 64s. and 4s. 2d. respectively, instructions were transmitted by the Secretary of State to the Governors of the several colonies in the West Indies, directing them to issue proclamations for the purpose of declaring the nominal rate of the doubloon, the dollar, and the

British shilling, in terms of the currency of those several colonies, according to the proportions and relative value of these coins fixed in Her Majesty's proclamation.

No instructions on this head were transmitted to the North American colonies, nor any subsidiary proclamations issued. In so far as related to the currency of those colonies, the proclamation was nugatory and inoperative. The only effect produced by it was an alteration in the rates at which the doubloon and the dollar were issued in the pay of the troops.

In the following year, however, that is to say, in the year 1839, two Acts were passed by the legislatures of Lower and Upper Canada, for regulating the rates and value of the several gold and silver coins mentioned therein.

The ordinance passed in Lower Canada, after reciting that the rates and value assigned to the several coins therein-mentioned are inconsistent with each other, and in many cases erroneous; and that it is highly desirable to establish a legal proportion between the pound sterling as represented by the British sovereign, and the pound currency of the province; and, as far as circumstances will permit, to assimilate the currency thereof to that of the mother country, but without injuriously affecting the interests of any party to any existing contracts, proceeds to enact—that a certain act passed in the 48th. Geo. III., entitled "An Act for "better regulating the weights and rates at which "certain coins shall pass current in the province, "&c.," shall be suspended during the time this ordinance shall be in force.

Although in the preamble of this ordinance it is alleged, that it is desirable that the currency of the province should be assimilated to that of the mother country, yet, in retaining the rate of 5s for the dollar, and assigning to the sovereign the rate of 1l. 4s. 4d., and proportionate rates to other gold coins, the framers of the ordinance appear to have had in view, and to have adopted, the proportion of fine silver to fine gold fixed by the Mint law of the United States, that is to say, 16 to 1, being about $1\frac{1}{2}$ per cent. below the proportion which prevails in the general market of the commercial world.

The ground for adopting the United States' proportion was probably an apprehension, that if the proportion that obtains in the general market were adopted, the gold coins would leave the colony and be exported to the States.

If such an apprehension existed, it was without any just foundation; for the over-valuation of gold in the States of the Union, must make gold the principal measure of property and exchange in that country, and to establish a premium in silver equal to the difference between the legal proportions in the United States, and the market proportions else-where. Hence, the probability is, that if the pro-portion of 16 to 1 had been adopted in Canada, the silver dollar would have been exported rather than the gold coins.

The rates assigned to the several coins of gold and silver, which it was ordained should pass current and be a legal tender, were as follows:—

	£.	s.	d.
Sovereign	1	4	4
United States' old eagle . . .	2	13	4
,, new eagle . .	2	10	0
Doubloon	3	17	8
French 40-franc piece . . .	1	18	7
Dollar	0	5	0
British crown	0	6	0
,, half-crown	0	3	0
,, shilling	0	1	3
,, sixpence	0	0	7½
,, groat	0	0	5

By these rates, not only was the proportionate value of the dollar, the doubloon, and the sovereign made to differ from the proportion established by Her Majesty's proclamation of the 13th September, 1838, but the rates assigned to British silver coins were not properly adjusted to either the one or the other, or to each other.

By the Upper Canada Act, all former Acts regulating the value of gold and silver coins in the province were repealed.

It was further enacted, that the gold coins mentioned in a schedule annexed to the Act, shall be deemed a legal tender at the rates and value set opposite to them in the schedule.

The rates assigned to the gold coins, in the schedule, were as follows:—

	£.	s.	d.
Sovereign	1	4	4
United States' eagle . . .	2	10	0
Doubloon	3	17	$8\frac{4}{16}$
French 40-franc piece . .	1	18	$6\frac{48}{100}$

It was enacted, that the silver coins specified in the schedule shall pass current and be a legal tender at the following rates :—

	s.	d.
Spanish, Mexican, Columbian, and United States' dollar	5	0
British crown	6	0
,, half-crown	3	0
,, shilling	1	3
,, sixpence	0	$7\frac{1}{2}$
French crown . . . . . , . . .	4	$8\frac{1}{2}\frac{1}{10}$

The rates and value assigned to the gold coins of Great Britain, France, and the United States, were very nearly the same as those adopted by the Legislature of Lower Canada; the rates and value assigned to the dollar, and to British silver coins, were exactly the same in both Acts; in both, the rates and value assigned to the different coins specified in the Acts were erroneous, and inconsistent with each other.

These Acts having a suspending clause, never came into operation, and did not receive the royal assent.

In the year 1841, an Act was passed by the

united Legislature of Canada, which appears to have
been framed with the view of correcting the
errors and imperfections of the ordinances above-
mentioned.

This Act, after reciting that, by the several Acts
now in force, in the respective portions of the province, the relative value of the gold and silver
coins, therein current, has not been accurately
established; and that the comparative value of the
pound sterling, and the pound in Halifax currency,
is inaccurately described, proceeds to enact, that
from and after the date of the Act, the several
Acts and ordinances therein mentioned, and all
other Acts, or parts of Acts, relating to the value
of gold, silver, and copper coins current by law in
either of the sections of the province, or in any
way relating to the currency and to the provisions
of this Act, shall be repealed.

It is then enacted, that the pound currency shall
be such that the pound sterling, as represented by
the British sovereign of the weight and fineness
now fixed by the laws of the United Kingdom,
shall be equal to, and any such British sovereign
shall be a legal tender for, 1*l.* 4*s.* 4*d.* currency.

As this enactment is the basis on which the rates
assigned to the different gold and silver coins
mentioned in the Act are determined, and according to which they are directed to be current
and a legal tender, the correctness of those rates
must be tried by a reference to it.

Those rates are stated and described in the Act as follows:—

GOLD COINS.

	£.	s.	d.
Eagle of the United States, coined before July 1, 1834, and weighing 11 dwts. 6 grs.	2	13	4
Eagle coined since July 1, 1834, and weighing 10 dwts. 18 grs.	2	10	0
Gold coins of France, and multiples and divisions thereof, in sums not less than 50l. currency . . . . per ounce	4	13	1
Old doubloon of Spain, Mexican and Chilian doubloon, and the parts thereof, in sums not less than 50l. currency . per ounce	4	9	7
Gold coins of La Plata and Columbia, in sums not less than 50l. currency, per oz.	4	9	5
Gold coins of Portugal and Brazil, in sums not less than 50l. currency . per ounce	4	14	6

SILVER COINS.

	£.	s.	d.
Milled dollar of Spain, the dollar of the United States, and of the several states of Peru, Chili, Central America, and the states of South America and Mexico, not weighing less than 17 dwts. 4 grs. . .	0	5	1
The half dollar of the same nations and governments	0	2	$6\frac{1}{2}$

The dollar and half dollar to be a legal tender to any amount.

	s.	d.
The quarter dollar	1	3
The eighth of a dollar . . .	0	$7\frac{1}{2}$
The sixteenth of a dollar . .	0	$3\frac{1}{2}$

The subdivisions of the dollar being less than halves thereof, to be a legal tender by tale to the amount of fifty shillings currency, and no more, until they shall have lost 1-25th of their proportionate weight of 17 dwts. 4 grs. respectively, after which they shall not be legal money.

The five-franc piece of France, weighing not less than 16 dwts., to be a legal tender to any amount.

The British crown . . . 6s. 1d.

All other divisions of the silver coins of the United Kingdom, of proportionate sums, to be a legal tender, to the extent of fifty shillings currency, and no more.

The old and new eagle of the United States, and the British sovereign, which are correctly rated with reference to each other, are the only gold coins which are declared by the Act to be a legal tender of payment *by tale*, at the rates respectively assigned to them. The gold coins of France, Spain, Mexico, Chili, La Plata, and Columbia are declared to be a legal tender *by weight*, in sums not less than 50l. currency, at rates which very nearly correspond with the rate of 1l. 4s. 4d. assigned to the sovereign.

The British silver crown is correctly rated with reference to the sovereign. The dollar of Spain, Peru, Chili, Central America, South America, and Mexico, assuming its value, in English money, to be 4s. 2d., is over-rated, with reference to the sovereign, one-sixth of a penny. The dollar of the United States, although about the half of one per cent. worse than the dollar of the New States of

Mexico and South America, has the same rate assigned to it as the dollar of those States.

These small discrepancies will give a slight ascendancy of the dollars and half-dollars of the United States over the dollars of Mexico and South America, in the circulation of the province.

The par of exchange—gold against gold—between Canada and Great Britain is 121*l*. 13*s*. 4*d*. of Canada currency for 100*l*. sterling; but as in computations of exchange with England, the old valuation of the dollar at 4*s*. 6*d*., and the Halifax denomination of 5*s*., are still adhered to, and at 121*l*. 13*s*. 4*d*. contain the same number of dollars, reckoning the dollar at 5*s*., as are contained in 109*l*. 10*s*., reckoning the dollar at 4*s*. 6*d*., the par of exchange with England is called 109*l*. 10*s*. The computation may be stated as follows :—

	£.	s.	d.
English money . . .	100	0	0
Premium	9	10	0
9)109	10	0
	12	3	4
£ 121	13	4

The sum of 121*l*. 13*s*. 4*d*. of Canada currency, or 100 sovereigns, is equal to 48·665* eagles or 486·65 dollars of the United States, which 486·65

* An eagle contains 232·$\frac{2}{10}$ of fine gold. 100 sovereigns contain 11300·1 grains of fine gold.

$$\frac{11300 \cdot 1}{232 \cdot 2} = 48 \cdot 665$$

dollars at 4s. 6d. (the rate assumed in the United States in computations of exchange with England), amount to £109·496., United States currency. Hence 100l. sterling = 121l. 13s. 4d. Canada currency = 486·65 gold dollars, or £109·496 currency of the United States.

The computation of the exchange between Canada, England, and the United States, is more complicated with reference to silver than to gold.

In England the basis of the currency is gold. It is so likewise in the United States; for although the United States' Mint is open to the public for the coinage of both metals to an unlimited extent, yet as the gold coins are over-rated with reference to those of silver, the former are the cheaper tender of payment, and therefore, the principal measure of property and exchange.

The metallic money of Canada consists of a mixture of gold and silver coins, adjusted to each other, according to the value of the two metals relatively to each other in the general market of the commercial world.

Now, assuming that the value of a Spanish, Mexican, or South American dollar, expressed in terms of the gold currency of Great Britain, is 4s. 2d., and making allowance for the over-valuation of one-sixth of a penny in the Canada currency Act of 1841, that is, assuming the rate of the silver dollar in Canada to be 5s. 0⅙d., the par of exchange with England is the same in silver as in gold, that is to say, 121*l.* 13*s.* 4*d.* currency for 100*l.* sterling.

But in the currency of Canada, the same rate is assigned to the silver dollar of the United States, as is assigned to the dollar of the New States of Mexico and South America, although the weight of the former is 412½, containing 371¼ grains of fine silver, while the latter contains on an average, 373 grains of fine silver. The dollar of the United States is, therefore, worse than the Mexican dollar by about the half of one per cent., or one-fourth of a penny sterling.

Hence, the par of exchange with England— silver against gold—is 122*l.* 5*s.* 6*d.* currency for 100*l.* sterling, or 10$\frac{1}{20}$*l.* premium.

Nova Scotia.

Previous to the year 1834 the rates at which the coins in circulation in this Province were current, were merely conventional. No proclamation of the Crown, nor any public enactment, existed, by which those rates, and the relative value of the coins, were settled and determined. But in that year an Act was passed (Provincial Act 4 Wm. IV., c. 61), the principal enactments and provisions of which were as follows:—

" Whereas the adoption of British sterling money " in the currency and moneys of account, of and " throughout all Her Majesty's dominions would be

" highly useful, and tend to unite more closely the
" interests of the colonies with those of the mother
" country. But to make such alteration in the
" currency of this Province, at present, would be
" inconvenient and inexpedient, unless the same
" were adopted in the adjoining Provinces : and
" whereas, in the meantime, and until such change
" shall be made in the currency of other colonies,
" it is requisite and necessary to establish a standard
" of value and equivalent for property, which may
" be obtained by fixing a value upon foreign gold and
" British silver coins : Be it therefore enacted, that,
" from and after the passing of this Act, the several
" British silver coins hereinafter mentioned and spe-
" cified, shall and may be offered, received, paid, and
" legally tendered by and to the Provincial Treasurer,
" or other public officer, or by or to any body politic
" or corporate, person or persons whomsoever, in
" payment, satisfaction, or discharge of any debt, sum
" of money, duties, contracts, obligations, liabilities,
" or demands whatsoever, at the several rates of value
" following : that is to say, the English shilling at
" the rate of 1s. 3d. currency, and the English six-
" pence at the rate of 7½d. currency, provided that no
" person shall be receiver, in one payment, of more
" than 50s. Halifax currency, in British silver coins,
" at the rate or rates aforesaid. And whereas Spanish
" American doubloons are brought into the Pro-
" vince in the course of trade, and in payment of the
" exports therefrom, and have been, since the year
" 1819, received and paid at and after the rate of

" 4_l._ currency; and four Treasury notes of 1_l._ each
" have since that time been deemed equivalent to
" one doubloon, and the difficulty of procuring
" British coins in the ordinary course of trade still
" continuing, it is necessary that the said doubloon
" should become and be made a legal tender at the
" rate aforesaid : Be it, therefore, enacted, &c., that,
" from and after the passing of this Act, the said
" doubloon, being of full weight and fineness, shall
" and may be offered and received, and paid, and
" legally tendered to the Provincial Treasurer, or
" other public officer, or by or to any body politic,
" or person or persons whomsoever, in payment,
" satisfaction, or discharge of any debt, sum of
" money, duties, obligations, liabilities, or demands
" contracted since the 19th day of April, 1819, at
" and after the rate of 4_l._ currency for one doubloon.
" And be it enacted, that the pound sterling, as re-
" presented by the gold coin of the United King-
" dom of Great Britain and Ireland, called the
" sovereign, shall henceforth be deemed and taken
" to be the unit or standard, or measure of money,
" or value whereby, or with reference to which all
" contracts which shall be entered into for the pay-
" ment of British sterling money, shall be regulated
" and ascertained within this Province."

It was " further enacted that the copper money of
" the United Kingdom, and copper coins procured by
" the Legislature for the use of the Province, shall
" be current at the same rate as British penny and
" halfpenny pieces, when payment is to be made in

" sterling money ; but if payment is to be made in
" the existing currency, then in like proportion, as
" such currency as is adjusted in the Act, bears to
" sterling money."

This Act expired on the 31st of December, 1835,
and was not afterwards renewed; but, in the year
1836, an Act was passed by the Legislature of this
Province (6 Wm. IV., c. 41), by which it was
enacted, that all duties imposed by the Act shall be
reduced into the currency of the Province, as follows: that is to say, all the several duties in the
first and second columns of the schedule contained
in the Act, shall be considered to be imposed in
sterling money of Great Britain, and the same shall
be converted into currency by adding to the aggregate amount of the duty one-fourth of the said
aggregate amount; and in calculating duties imposed on articles according to the value thereof,
100*l.* sterling shall be taken to represent 125*l.* currency. It is further enacted, that duties may be
received in Treasury notes, at the rate of 20*s.* for
1*l.* currency; in doubloons of the rate of 4*l.* currency; in British coins at the rate of 25*s.* for each
sovereign, and in like proportion for silver coins;
provided that no greater sum than 2*l.* currency
shall be received and paid in British silver coins at
any one time.

At the date of the last-mentioned Act, the conventional rates assigned to the several coins in circulation in Nova Scotia were as follows :—

	£.	s.	d.	
Doubloon	4	0	0	currency.
American eagle	2	10	0	,,
Sovereign	1	5	0	,,
Dollar of Mexico, South America,				
and the United States . . .	0	5	0	,,
English crown	0	6	3	,,
English shilling	0	1	3	,,
English sixpence	0	0	7½	,,

According to those rates, the American eagle
and the dollar of Spain, Mexico, South America,
and the United States were under-valued with reference to the doubloon, and to the gold and silver
coins of Great Britain.

This defect was remedied by an Act passed by
the Legislature of the Province, in the year 1842,
by which it is enacted, that the doubloon being of
not less weight than 415 grains, shall be a legal
tender for four pounds currency, the soverign for
twenty-five shillings currency; and that for all
debts and obligations contracted in sterling money,
the doubloon shall be a legal tender for sixty-four
shillings, and the sovereign for one pound; that
the Peruvian, Mexican, and old Spanish dollar,
being of the full weight of 416 grains, and containing not less than 373 grains of pure silver,
shall be a legal tender at the rate of four shillings
and twopence sterling, or five shillings and two-
pence-halfpenny currency; that all British silver
coins shall be a legal tender at the proportionate
rates which they respectively bear to that of the
sovereign, but for no greater amount at one

time than fifty shillings currency; and that the pence and halfpence legally current in the United Kingdom, and the copper coins procured by the authority of the Legislature for the use of, and issued by the Treasury of the Province, shall be current, as penny and halfpenny pieces currency, but for no greater amount at one time than twelve-pence currency.

The rates assigned by this Act to the doubloon, the dollar, and to British gold and silver coins, agree with the proportions fixed by Her Majesty's proclamation of the 13th September, 1838. The real par of exchange with England is now 125*l.* currency for 100*l.* sterling; or, according to the American mode of computation, 12½ per cent. premium on sterling money.

New Brunswick.

Various Acts have, at different times, been passed by the Legislature of this Province for regulating and determining the rate and value at which certain British and foreign coins shall pass current, and be received as a legal tender.

The rates so determined were as follows:—

	£.	s.	d.
Spanish milled dollar (26 Geo. III.) . .	0	5	0
French crown (26 Geo. III.)	0	5	6
Portugese Johannes (45 Geo. III.) . .	4	0	0
,, Moidores (45 Geo. III.) . .	1	0	0
French Louis d'or (45 Geo. III.) . . .	1	2	6

	£.	s.	d.
French Pistole (45 Geo. III.)	0	18	0
Spanish milled doubloon (60 Geo. III.) .	3	14	0
English guinea (60 Geo III.)	1	3	4
,, sovereign (60 Geo. III.) . . .	1	2	3
United States' eagle (60 Geo. III.) . .	2	10	0
English crown of the new coinage (60 Geo. III.)	0	5	6
United States' dollar	0	5	0

When the 60 Geo. III. (anno 1820) was passed, the eagle of the United States' weighed 11 dwts. 6 grains, and contained $247\frac{1}{2}$ grains of fine gold. By a new regulation of the United States Mint, in 1834, the fine gold contained in an eagle was reduced from $247\frac{1}{2}$ grains to $232\frac{2}{10}$ grains. Notwithstanding this alteration, the gold eagle of the United States continued to pass current at the rate of fifty shillings, assigned to it by the Act above-mentioned.

In the Acts above referred to, the gold and silver coins of Great Britain, being greatly undervalued with reference to the American eagle and the dollar, were not current at the rates assigned to them by law, but varied in price, according to the varying state of the exchange with England. The only coins that could be retained in circulation, at the rates assigned to them, were the American eagle and half eagle, the dollar, and the French crown. With the exception of the last-mentioned coin, of which the quantity in circulation was inconsiderable, the currency of New

Brunswick rested, therefore, on the same metallic basis as that of the United States of America.

In the United States, the gold coins being more highly valued with reference to the silver dollar than consists with the relative value of the two metals in the general market of the world. frequently bear a small premium. For the same reason, silver dollars were with difficulty retained in circulation in New Brunswick.

With a view to remove the difficulties created by the erroneous and disproportionate rates assigned to different gold and silver coins by the several provincial Acts above-mentioned, an Act was passed in the year 1843, which enacted that from and after the passing of the Act the coins therein enumerated shall pass current, and be a legal tender, at the following rates:—

	£.	s.	d.
English sovereign . . .	1	4	2
French crown	0	5	6
English crown	0	6	0½
Dollar	0	5	0
American eagle	2	10	0

As the rates assigned by this Act to the several coins therein mentioned were not correctly adjusted to each other, with reference to the relative value of the coins, the Act, having a suspending clause, was not allowed to come into operation.

In the following year an Act was passed, entitled an Act to establish the value of certain

British coins in this province, and to amend the Acts relating to the establishment of a legal tender.

By this Act it is enacted that the first and second sections of an Act made and passed in the 58th year of the reign of King George III., and, also, so much of an Act passed in the 36th year of the reign of King George III., as shall be contrary to any of the provisions of this Act, shall be repealed.

The Act then enacts, that from and after the passing of the Act, the several coins therein enumerated, and the several respective aliquot parts thereof, shall pass current, and be received as a legal tender, at the following rates and valuation, that is to say, the English sovereign at one pound four shillings currency, the English crown at six shillings currency.

The coins now current in this province, of which the rates and value have been duly assigned by law, are the following :—

	£.	s.	d.
English sovereign	1	4	0
United States' eagle	2	10	0
Spanish, Mexican, South American, and			
United States' dollar	0	5	0
English crown, and the aliquot parts thereof,			
at proportionate rates	0	6	0

The eagle of the United States, containing 232 grains of fine gold, is over-valued with reference to the sovereign, containing 113 grains of fine gold, about 1½ per cent.; this coin should have been rated at 2*l.* 9*s.* 3*d.* currency.

Were it not for this over-valuation of the eagle, the currency of New Brunswick might conveniently be converted into sterling money, by deducting one-sixth from any given amount thereof.

The sterling value of the eagle and the dollar would then be 2*l.* 1*s.* 0½*d.*, and 4*s.* 2*d.* respectively.

Newfoundland.

In this island there exists no legal enactments for the regulation of its currency. The metallic money in circulation consists, principally, of silver dollars which are nominally rated at 5*s.* per dollar; and as the value of a dollar in sterling money is supposed in the colony to be 4*s.* 4*d.*, the par of exchange with England is called 115*l.* 7*s.* 8*d.* currency for 100*l.* sterling. In consequence of the over-valuation of the dollar in British money, bills on England generally bear a premium of 4 to 6 per cent.

No fixed rates in the currency of the colony are assigned to British silver coins; the shilling passes sometimes for 1*s.* 2*d.*, sometimes for 1*s.* 3*d.* currency, varying probably with the variations of the mercantile exchange with England. There is, consequently, great irregularity in the currency of the island; and the mode of transacting ordinary business (it is frequently effected by barter) is attended with much perplexity and inconvenience.

On the 22nd April, 1845, an Act was passed by the General Assembly of the island for regulating the currency.

In this Act it is enacted that the several coins enumerated in a schedule, thereunto annexed, shall be a legal tender for the sums specified in the schedule.

Those rates are as follows :—

	£.	s.	d.
Doubloon	3	16	9⅗
British sovereign . . .	1	4	0
Dollar	0	5	0
British crown	0	6	0
Half-crown	0	3	0
British shilling	0	1	2⅖

The foregoing rates are correctly adjusted to the current rate of five shillings assigned to the dollar ; but as the Act contained a clause ordaining that all sums of money payable by any local Act in sterling money, and all contracts made in the colony, and then subsisting, for the payment of money in sterling, shall be deemed to be satisfied and discharged by the payment of current money at the rate of 115l. 7s. 8d. thereof for 100l. sterling, it did not receive Her Majesty's assent.

If the enactment in this section of the Act had become the law of the island, this strange inconsistency would have ensued, namely, that a debt of one hundred pounds in sterling money might have been discharged with British gold and silver coins of the sterling value of 96*l*. 3*s*. 1*d*.

Bermuda.

When the Queen's proclamation of the 14th September, 1838, fixing the sterling value of the dollar at 4*s*. 2*d*., and of the doubloon at 64*s*., was published, the currency of Bermuda was nearly the same as that of Jamaica; the current rate of a dollar was 6*s*. 8*d*., and a doubloon was deemed equal to sixteen dollars.

At that time it was the practice of the House of Assembly, in framing their Acts for granting supplies, to declare that 100*l*. sterling shall signify 150*l*. currency. At the same time, the colonial treasurer required thirteen shillings sterling, or three dollars at 4*s*. 4*d*., for one pound currency, making 100*l*. sterling equal to 153*l*. 16*s*. 11*d*. currency. In the collection of powder duties, and in transactions between individuals, the British shilling was received and paid at the rate of four shillings to the dollar, making 100*l*. sterling equal to 166*l*. 13*s*. 4*d*. currency.

These discrepancies were owing to the confusion created by the assignment, in the colony, of the same current rate to the silver dollar as to the sixteenth of a gold doubloon; both were considered to be of the same value, and were comprehended under the same denomination, that is to say, three silver dollars, or three-sixteenths of a doubloon, made one pound currency.

The dollar being under-valued with reference to the doubloon, the latter coin became the principal measure of property, and the standard of exchange.

If, after the publication of Her Majesty's proclamation of the 14th September, 1838, it had been determined to retain the denominations of the island currency, it would have been necessary, in order to establish the circulation of the dollar, concurrently with that of the doubloon, to have raised the rate of the former coin from 6$s.$ 8$d.$ to 6$s.$ 11$\frac{1}{3}d.$, leaving the sale of the doubloon of 5$l.$ 6$s.$ 8$d.$ as before.

The island Legislature, however, took a better course. An Act was passed, ordaining that from and after the 1st January, 1842, all pecuniary contracts and engagements shall be entered into and executed according to the currency of the United Kingdom; and that all pecuniary contracts and engagements entered into according to the currency of the island, before the commencement of the Act, shall be discharged at the rate and in the proportion of 100$l.$ sterling for 166$l.$ 13$s.$ 4$d.$ of the present currency.

It was further enacted, that from and after the commencement of the Act, Spanish, Mexican, and Columbian doubloons, weighing not less than 17 dwts. 8 grs., shall be current at the rate of sixty-four shillings; and that Spanish, Mexican, and Columbian dollars shall be current at the rate of four shillings and twopence each.

Provision was made in the Act for the adjustment of the accounts of the colonial treasurer, and for the receipt in sterling money, or its equivalent in foreign coins, of all taxes and revenues of the Crown.

The currency of this island was thus judiciously placed upon a just and satisfactory foundation, without inconvenience, and without prejudice to existing contracts.

From the foregoing review of the origin and present state of the currency of the British provinces in North America, it will be seen that, although, with two trifling exceptions, the coins which are legally authorised ˏto be current in Canada, Nova Scotia, and New Brunswick, are proportionately rated according to the weight and fineness of the precious metals respectively contained in them, the nominal rates assigned to the same coins, are different in the different provinces.

Those rates are as follows :—

CANADA.

	£.	s.	d.
The sovereign	1	4	4
The shilling	0	1	2¼
The dollar . ˏ . . .	0	5	1

NOVA SCOTIA.

	£.	s.	d.
The doubloon	4	0	0
The sovereign	1	5	0
The shilling	0	1	3
The dollar	0	5	2½

NEW BRUNSWICK.

The sovereign	1	4	0
The shilling	0	1	2⅗
The dollar	0	5	0

These differences in the nominal rates assigned to the same coins in the three provinces above-mentioned, and the inconvenient fraction in the rate assigned to the British shilling in two of them, occasion much trouble and inconvenience in all computations of exchange with each other, and with the mother country, which trouble and inconvenience, it is very desirable, should, if possible, be obviated.

The most effectual way of getting rid of the difficulty would be to establish, in those colonies, British sterling denominations for British coins, and proportionate rates for those foreign coins of which it has been, or may be, deemed expedient to legalize the circulation.

To this end it would be necessary that enactments should be passed by the Colonial Legislatures, ordaining that from and after a day to be named, all pecuniary contracts and engagements shall be entered into according to the currency of the United Kingdom; and all pecuniary contracts and engagements entered into according to the currency of the province, before the commencement of the Act, shall be discharged at the rate and in the proportion of 100*l.* sterling for so much of the said currency as 100 sovereigns, rated in the terms of that currency, amount to.

No reasonable objection can be made to a change of this nature. No existing pecuniary contracts or obligations would be affected by it. No hindrance or difficulty in the way of the future commercial operations of those colonies—domestic or foreign— would result from it.

THE CURRENCY OF GIBRALTAR.

Accounts, at Gibraltar, are kept in dollars, reals, and quartos.

$$1 \text{ dollar} = 12 \text{ reals.}$$
$$1 \text{ real } = 16 \text{ quartos.}$$

The coins current in the garrison are the doubloons and dollars of *Spain*, and their sub-divisions, one doubloon being deemed equal to sixteen dollars. The quartos are copper coins of different countries, and are merely counters, or representatives of the aliquot parts of a dollar.

Previously to the year 1825, the duties and local revenue of Gibraltar were imposed and collected in Spanish money. In that year the Government gave directions for keeping the revenue accounts in sterling money.

In making this change, the rate assigned to the dollar, and to one-sixteenth of a doubloon, was four shillings and four-pence. Consequently, a person having duties to pay, although rated to those duties in sterling money, continued to pay precisely the same number of dollars or doubloons as he would have paid if no alteration in the mode of keeping the Government accounts had been made. The alteration, in so far as the collection of the revenue was concerned, was merely nominal.

In the year 1835, it was directed by a minute

of the Treasury Board, that the rate of 69s. 4d. (4s. 4d. × 16) assigned to the doubloon, should be reduced to 66s.

Against this alteration the merchants of Gibraltar remonstrated, observing, that in that garrison, although the gold and the silver dollar occasionally vary in value relatively to each other, yet that in all ordinary cases, payments are made indifferently in the one or the other; and that if the rate of the gold coins were lowered, when tendered for duties nominally reserved in sterling money, the payer of the duties would be deprived of the option which he had, previously, enjoyed of paying duties and discharging other obligations in either gold or silver, at the rates which have long existed in Spain and Gibraltar.

This subject was again brought under the consideration of the Lords of the Treasury, and it was determined to rescind the order of 1835, in so far as relates to Gibraltar, thereby leaving the doubloon and the dollar to be issued from the military chest, and in payment of duties at the rates, relatively to each other, which had previously prevailed in the garrison, and which still prevail in the kingdom of Spain.

Soon after the publication of Her Majesty's Proclamation of the 14th September, 1838, an application was made by the Governor of Gibraltar to the Secretary of State for the Colonies, for the extension to the troops stationed at that garrison, the same regulation with regard to their pay, as had been made with respect to the pay of the troops stationed in North America and the West Indies, namely, the issue of the doubloon at 64*s.*, and the dollar at 4*s.* 2*d.*

It was found, however, on inquiry, that the two cases were not similar.

At Gibraltar, the only recognized tenders of payment are the doubloon and dollar of *Spain.* In the West Indies, the doubloon and dollar of Mexico and South America are a legal tender of payment.

The doubloon, which at Gibraltar is deemed equal to 16 dollars, is deemed in the West Indies equal only to $15\frac{36}{100}$ dollars.

At Gibraltar, the dollar being under-valued with reference to the doubloon, is practically excluded from the ordinary channels of the currency, and generally bears a premium of $2\frac{1}{2}$ to 3 per cent.

It thus appears that the money of Gibraltar, in so far as doubloons and dollars are concerned, differs from that of the West Indies in two important particulars.

First. The old Spanish doubloon and the old Spanish dollar (commonly called the pillar dollar) only are recognized as the legal money of the garrison ; while the doubloon and the dollar of Mexico and South America are not ordinarily current there, but are purchased and sold in the market as bullion.

Second. The law which in Spain makes sixteen dollars the equivalent of a doubloon, obtains likewise at Gibraltar.

On the first point it is to be observed, that the old Spanish doubloon, although of the same weight and fineness as the doubloon of Mexico and South America, is deemed at Gibraltar, as well as in some other parts of the world, to be of superior value compared with the latter.

This superior estimation in which the Spanish doubloon is held, probably arises from some prejudice which exists in its favour, and from its comparative scarcity.

One of the consequences of this artificial or extrinsic value of the Spanish doubloon, is the high comparative rate of exchange which generally prevails at Gibraltar upon London. In the three years, 1838, 1839, and 1840, the average rate at which bills were negotiated by the Commissariat at Gibraltar, on the Treasury, was 66s. 8d. per doubloon; whereas, if Mexican and South American doubloons had been the basis of the currency of the garrison, the average rate of exchange probably would not have exceeded 64s. per doubloon.

When the doubloon was issued by the Commissary for the pay of the troops at Gibraltar, at the rate of 69s. 4d., the dissatisfaction of the latter with the mode in which they received their pay was, in a great degree, owing to a circumstance which it is necessary to explain.

According to the monetary regulations of Gibraltar, one sixteenth of a doubloon is divided into 192 quartos.* When the sixteenth of a doubloon is reckoned equal to 4s. 4d., 192 quartos should likewise be reckoned equal to 4s. 4d.; or, which is the same thing, 12 quartos should be reckoned equal to 13 British pence, and 1 quarto to $1\frac{1}{12}$ British farthings.

Now these small fractions are not easily managed by the pay-sergeant, in the statement of his account with the soldier. In that account the soldier is charged with the disbursements made on his behalf, and the balance of his pay is paid to him in money. In order to avoid small fractions, the pay-sergeant charged the money so paid, not at the rate of 4s. 4d. for one-sixteenth of a doubloon, or $1\frac{1}{12}$ farthings for 1 quarto, but at the rate of 4s. for one-sixteenth of a doubloon, or one farthing for one quarto ; and in order that the pay-sergeant might obtain compensation for the difference, a further charge of one penny on every 48 quartos was periodically made, under the head of "currency," or difference of exchange.

The consequence of this mode of keeping the account was, that the soldier was led to suppose that a Spanish quarto, or the $\frac{1}{192}$ part of a gold dollar, and a British farthing, or the $\frac{1}{960}$ part of a gold sovereign, are really of the same value, and

* At Cadiz the dollar is divided into $10\frac{5}{8}$ reals, making the dollar equal to 170 quartos.

that the charge of one penny on every shilling, under the head of " currency," was a charge to which he was not fairly liable.

If it had happened that, in the money of account at Gibraltar, the dollar, or the one-sixteenth of a doubloon, had been divided into 208, instead of 192 quartos, it is probable that no complaint on this score would have arisen.

In this view of the case, it will be seen that the complaint made by the troops at Gibraltar, of the charge under the head of " currency," was destitute of all just foundation.

But although in this respect the troops had no just ground of complaint, yet, as the sterling rate assigned to the Spanish doubloon was higher than the average rate of exchange at which bills on the Treasury were negotiated for that coin, and as the troops at foreign stations have a just claim to receive their pay in foreign coins rated according to their sterling value, the Lords of Her Majesty's Treasury were pleased to direct that the rate at which the doubloon shall in future be issued to the troops at Gibraltar shall be reduced from 69s. 4d. to 66s. 8d., or 4s. 2d. the gold dollar.

It should be observed, however, that this alteration in the sterling rate of the Spanish doubloon will not altogether remove the misconception occasioned by the mode in which the soldier's account is stated to him by the pay-sergeant. If that mode be continued, the only effect, in this respect, produced by the alteration, will be a reduction of the charge under the head of currency, from one penny per shilling to one halfpenny per shilling.

A different mode of stating the soldier's monthly accounts would, in all probability, remove this source of misconception.

By an order of Her Majesty in Council, dated the 3rd September, 1844, the Order in Council of the 23rd March, 1825, was revoked in so far as respects the garrison and territory of Gibraltar; and a Proclamation was issued, directing that in the said garrison and territory the doubloon and the gold and silver dollar of Spain, Mexico, and South America shall circulate and be received in payment as being of the full value and equivalent to current money of the United Kingdom, at the following rates :—

	£.	s.	d.
The doubloon at	3	6	8
The dollar at	0	4	2

By a subsequent Proclamation, dated the 26th April, 1845, the rate assigned, in the last-mentioned Proclamation, to the doubloon of Spain, Mexico, and South America, was confined to the doubloon of Spain only.

THE CURRENCY OF MALTA.

Accounts, at Malta, are kept in scudi, tari, and grains.

> 1 scudi = 12 tari.
> 1 tari = 20 grains.

Previously to the year 1825, the coins in circulation in the island consisted chiefly of—

> Spanish pillar dollars.
> Imperial and Sicilian dollars.
> Maltese silver coins.

From the regulations which have at different times been made at Malta, with respect to the value of the gold doubloon of Spain, it appears that, previously to the year 1824, the rate, in Maltese currency, assigned to the Spanish dollar, was 30 tari.

On 6th January, 1801, a notification was published, ordering that the Spanish doubloon shall be received at 16 dollars each, and cannot be refused by any one at that rate.

On the 10th of the same month, the Lieutenant-Governor directed that, in order to prevent any misunderstanding or dispute, the Spanish doubloon shall be regulated at 16 dollars of 30 tari each, and no more, and that the doubloon shall be universally received by all at forty scudi of Malta.

It was afterwards deemed expedient to reduce the current rate of the Spanish doubloon to $15\frac{1}{2}$ dollars, that is to say, to 38 scudi and 9 tari of Malta ($15\frac{1}{2}$ dollars of 30 tari=38 scudi 9 tari);

and on the 21st October, 1801, a Proclamation was published to that effect.

On the 10th June, 1824, a Proclamation was issued for establishing the rate of the Spanish dollar at 31 tari 10 grains.

By this Proclamation the rate, in Maltese currency, assigned to the Spanish dollar, was raised 5 per cent.

On the 9th June, 1825, a Proclamation was issued, as follows :—

" His Honour the Lieutenant-Governor is pleased to " enact that, from and after the 24th instant, the British " silver and copper coins hereinafter enumerated shall " pass current in the Island of Malta and its dependencies, " at the following rates respectively, of Maltese currency, " viz.—

SILVER.

	Scudi.	tari.	grs.		grs.
The crown	3	0	0	or	720
The half-crown	1	6	0	,,	360
The shilling	0	7	4	,,	144
The sixpence	0	3	12	,,	72

COPPER.

The Penny	12
The Halfpenny	6
The Farthing	3

" In all payments to Government, the above-mentioned " British coins will be received at the Treasury and all " other public offices of the Government, at the rates " specified in Maltese currency, and issued in the same " manner.

" His Honour is pleased further to notify, that the " measure above stated is preparatory to the general " introduction of the British metallic currency as the cir- " culating medium in these possessions."

On the 11th October, 1825, the Lieutenant-Governor published Her Majesty's Order in Council of the 25th March, 1825, relating to the circulation of British silver and copper money in the colonies, and caused a Proclamation to be published, declaring that in the Island of Malta and its dependencies, engagements for the payment of money shall be dischargeable in British silver money, or in Spanish dollars, at the rate of 4s. 4d. each, at the option of the debtor, and repealing the Proclamation of the 10th June, 1824, fixing the current value of the Spanish dollar in Maltese currency ; which dollar, it was ordained, shall henceforth pass current, in exchange with Maltese currency, for the same amount, in that currency, as 4s. 4d. of the British silver money, the British metallic currency continuing to be equivalent in reference to, and in exchange with, the Maltese currency, at the rates specified in the Proclamation of the 9th June, 1825.

It thus appears that the rate of the Spanish dollar, in Maltese currency, was raised by the Proclamation of the 10th June, 1824, from 30 tari to $31\frac{1}{2}$ tari, or 5 per cent.; and that, by the Proclamation of the 9th June, 1825, that rate was reduced from $31\frac{10}{20}$ tari to $31\frac{4}{20}$ tari,* or about 1 per cent.

On the 27th May, 1834, a Proclamation was published, ordaining that, from and after the date

* 4s. 4d., at 144 tari per shilling, are 624 grains, or $31\frac{4}{20}$ tari.

thereof, " the dollar of the following states, " namely, Mexico, Peru, Bolivia, Chili, and Rio " Plata, shall pass current within these islands, at " the rate of 4s. 4d., British sterling money, being " the same rate at which the Spanish dollar is " now current in these possessions."

By an Order in Council, dated the 24th March, 1844, the above-mentioned Proclamation of the 9th June, 1825, was approved and confirmed; and the Proclamations of the 13th October, 1825, and the 27th May, 1834, were revoked and rescinded. At the same time, a Proclamation by the Queen was published, declaring and ordaining, that throughout the island of Malta and its dependencies, the dollar of Spain, Mexico, and the South American States, shall circulate and be received in payment, as being of the full value of 4s. 2d., sterling money of the United Kingdom; and that, in all payments to be made in the said island and its dependencies, tender of payment in the said coins shall be deemed and taken to be a lawful tender, in the same manner as if such tender had been made in the current coin of the United Kingdom.

The effect of this Proclamation was to reduce the rate of the dollar, in Maltese currency, to its former rate of 30 tari, leaving the rates assigned to British gold and silver in that currency unaltered.

The coins rated in Maltese currency, which are

now a legal tender of payment at Malta, are as follows:—

GOLD.

	Scudi.	tari.	grains.
Doubloon of Spain, Mexico, and South America	38	4	16
Sovereign	12	0	0

SILVER.

	Scudi.	tari.	grains.
Dollar of Spain, Mexico, and South America	2	6	0
Dollar of Sicily	2	4	16
Crown	3	0	0
Half-crown	1	6	0
Shilling	0	7	4
Sixpence	0	3	12

COPPER.

	Scudi.	tari.	grains.
Penny	0	0	12
Halfpenny	0	0	6
Farthing	0	0	3

The currency of Malta has given rise to much controversy, and has been greatly misunderstood. The introduction of British silver coins, and of the dollars of Mexico and South America, into the circulation of the island, has been represented, not only as having been prejudicial to its commercial interests, but as a fraud practised on its inhabitants by the Government.

These representations are destitute of all just foundation. It is desirable to trace, to its source, the misconception in which they appear to have originated.

First, with respect to the introduction of British silver coins:—

The rates assigned to those coins, in Maltese currency, being considerably higher, with reference to their intrinsic value, than the rates assigned to the dollar, and other silver coins, of which the metallic money of Malta previously consisted, the introduction of British silver money, it is alleged, displaced the more valuable coins, and depreciated the currency of the island to the extent of about 6 per cent.

No facts are adduced in support of this statement; on the contrary, it is admitted that when 4s. 4d. of British silver were legally current, at the same rate as a dollar, the former generally bore a premium, as against the latter. It is admitted, moreover, that since the first introduction of British silver into the circulation of Malta, the coins in circulation have consisted chiefly, not of British silver, but of foreign coins.

These admissions are wholly irreconcileable with the statement, that British silver coins have driven the more valuable coins from circulation, and depreciated the currency. The statement appears, indeed, to be rather an inference from an assumed general principle, than a statement of facts. It is assumed, that when coins, differing from each other in intrinsic value, are authoritatively put into circulation at the same rate or denomination, the superior coins will be driven abroad, and the inferior only will remain. Hence it is concluded, that the consequence which is stated to have actually occurred, must necessarily have taken place.

Now, not only are the facts of the case incorrectly stated, but the whole argument is built on an infirm basis. It is not true that the introduction of British silver coins into the circulation of Malta drove away the dollar, and other silver coins. It is not correct to say that coins of inferior intrinsic value will necessarily drive away the superior coins. The general proposition is true only on certain conditions, which conditions appear, in this case, to have been overlooked or disregarded. Of those conditions, the most important is, that the means and the opportunity shall exist of converting, readily and without delay, without any seignorage or mint-charge, and without any loss of weight or fineness, uncoined silver into the over-rated coin, and that, consequently, the coins shall always be of the same exchangeable value as that of the metal of which they are made.

Now, with respect to British silver coins, those conditions are altogether wanting. No one can obtain those coins at the British Mint in exchange for the same quantity of silver as that of which the coins are made; nor, indeed, obtain them there at all, without the express permission and authority of the Government.

The amount thrown into circulation being thus limited, those coins derive an extrinsic value from their scarcity ;* which extrinsic value, if the Mint were open to the public for their coinage, they would cease to possess.

The question then is, how is that exact degree of scarcity—that limit to the supply, which is necessary to sustain the value of British silver coins at a given point—to render 20 English shillings of the same exchangeable value as a sovereign, correctly ascertained?

The answer to this question is, that the amount of silver coins fabricated at, and issued from the British Mint, is properly determined and regulated by the Government. Experience has amply proved that the judgment and discretion of the Government, in this respect, may be so exercised as to preserve the value of the silver coins at its proper level, and to prevent the inconvenience either of deficiency or of excess. Neither the prices of gold and silver, nor the foreign exchanges, have been in any way acted on or affected by the silver coins.

It may perhaps be said, that the sole legal tender of payment, in Great Britain, being the sovereign, and the silver coins being used only as tokens, for the convenience of change, the latter are subsidiary and subordinate to the gold coins;

* " It is on this principle that paper money circulates; the whole charge for paper money may be considered as seignorage. Though it has no intrinsic value, yet by limiting its quantity, its value in exchange is as great as an equal denomination of coin, or of bullion in that coin."
—Ricardo's Political Economy, 3rd ed., p. 422.

whereas, in the colonies, the silver coins being a legal tender to an unlimited amount, are there a principal measure of property and exchange.

This is true. It may, however, safely be affirmed that if, in Great Britain, the limitation of the legal tender to 40s. were wholly abrogated and rescinded, neither the Bank of England, nor any person or body of persons, would discharge their pecuniary engagements more advantageously with silver than with gold coins, so long as the issue of silver coins is restrained and limited, as it has heretofore been, by the Government.

Now this is the case in the colonies.

In those colonies where the legalized coins are properly adjusted to each other, and to sterling money, with reference to their respective exchange-able value, no advantage accrues to a debtor, no loss is sustained by a creditor, in consequence of payment of the debt being made in British silver coins rather than in dollars. At Malta, indeed, when 4s. 4d. in British silver, and a dollar, passed current at the same rate or the same nominal value, a creditor, instead of being injured, was really benefited by such payment, inasmuch as the dollar, with reference to sterling money was over-rated 4 per cent.

The allegation, then, that the introduction of British silver coins depreciated the currency of Malta, and inflicted an injury on its inhabitants, is utterly groundless.

It is alleged, secondly, that the establishment of
the legal tender of the dollar of Mexico and South
America, at the same rate as the Spanish dollar,
injured the commerce of the island, by banishing
the latter from circulation, and substituting for it
an inferior and objectionable coin.

The principal objection urged against the Mexican dollar is the irregularity of its weight.

Now, this objection is not less applicable to the
Spanish pillar dollar than to the Mexican dollar.
Of 100 Spanish dollars weighed individually and
separately, at the Bank of England, it was found
that the lightest weighed 16 dwts. 14 grs., and
the heaviest 17 dwts. 18 grs., and the average of
each dollar was 17 dwts. 6 grs. Of the same
number of Mexican, the lightest was 16 dwts. 16 grs.,
and the heaviest 18 dwts. 3 grs., the average weight
of each of the 100 dollars being 17 dwts. $8\frac{7}{10}$ grs.

It was not, then, to the greater irregularity in the
weights of Mexican and South American dollars,
compared with the weights of Spanish dollars,
nor yet to the less average weight of the former
compared with the average weight of the latter,
that the alleged inferiority of the Mexican and
South American dollars could be justly ascribed.
It is true, however, that the introduction of the
latter coin into the circulation of Malta, expelled
the former.

Of this fact, the correct explanation is to be
found in the prejudice which exists amongst the

people, in certain parts of the Mediterranean, in favour of the Spanish dollar, and in its comparative scarcity. The same prejudice prevails in China. The dollars of the coinage of Carolus are preferred to those of the coinage of Ferdinand ; and both are more highly estimated than the dollars of Mexico and South America.

This prejudice, it may be expected, will at length wear away. But if that should not be the case, it must surely be allowed, that a coin which is no longer fabricated, which is gradually becoming more and more scarce, and which must in no very long time wholly disappear from the field of commerce, is a very unfit instrument to be the measure of property and of exchange.

The dollars of Mexico and South America, on the other hand, are worth neither more nor less than the silver of which they are made ; and may always be obtained, at all the principal marts of commerce, in sufficient abundance for the purposes for which they are required.

It has already been stated, that in the year before the royal Proclamation of the 25th March, 1825, fixing the rate of the Spanish dollar in the colonies at 4s. 4d. sterling, was promulgated, namely in the year 1824, the Lieutenant-Governor issued a Proclamation by which the rate of the dollar, in Maltese currency was fixed at 31 tari 10 grains. The original value assigned to that coin appears to have been 30 tari. The effect of the last-mentioned Proclamation, therefore, was to raise the rate of the dollar, or, in other words, to depreciate the currency of Malta to the extent of 5 per cent.

The Proclamation of the Lieutenant-Governor, issued on the 9th June, 1825, fixed the rate of the British shilling at 7 tari 4 grains; and as, by a subsequent Proclamation, dated 11th October, 1825, it was ordained that the dollar shall thenceforth pass current at 4s. 4d. sterling, the rate of the dollar became fixed at 31 tari 4 grains.

In consequence of this over-valuation of the dollar, with reference to sterling money, the intention of the Government to establish the metallic money of Great Britain, as the circulating medium of Malta, was frustrated, and it became necessary, in order to realize that intention, to reduce the rate of the dollar from 31 tari 4 grains to its original rate of 30 tari.

This was accomplished by the Queen's Proclamation of the 4th March, 1844, by which it was ordained that the dollar of Mexico and South America shall circulate and be received in payment throughout the island of Malta and its dependencies, as being of the full value of, and equivalent to, 4s. 2d. sterling money of the United Kingdom; for, as by the Proclamation of the Lieutenant-Governor, dated the 9th June, 1825, it was ordained that the British shilling shall pass current for 7 tari 4 grains, the current value of 4s. 2d., under that regulation, was 30 tari of Malta.

The dollar of Sicily still continued conventionally to pass current at 30 tari, or 4s. 2d. sterling.

This coin was found, on assay at the British Mint, to contain, on an average, 14 dwts. 17·45 grains of pure silver, of which the value, at 5s. per ounce of British standard silver, is 3s. $11\frac{88}{100}d$.

A Royal Proclamation was afterwards issued, ordaining that the dollar of Sicily shall pass current and be deemed a legal tender within the island of Malta, and its dependencies, at the rate of four shillings sterling, equal to 28 tari 16 grains in Maltese currency.

The measures which the Government has deemed it necessary to adopt, with regard to the currency of Malta, are clearly described and satisfactorily vindicated in a despatch, dated 23rd May, 1845, from Lord Stanley to Governor Lieut-General Sir P. Stuart, of which despatch the following are extracts ;—

" It has been the object of Her Majesty's Government, " in these arrangements, to provide both for the defective " state of the local currency, arising from the circulation " of dollars of insufficient weight, and for a more effectual " assimilation of the standard of value at Malta to that " of the United Kingdom, which may be considered as " the legitimate standard for Her Majesty's colonial " possessions.

" As the want of ready access to supplies of British

" coin might, occasionally, give rise to inconvenience
" from scarcity of metallic circulating medium, if foreign
" coins were excluded from legalized currency at Malta,
" such exclusion has not appeared to be advisable; but
" as the correction of any over-valuation of Spanish or
" South American dollars, or of any other foreign coins
" circulating in the island, would be a necessary prelimi-
" nary to the attainments of either of the objects before
" adverted to, the rate at which Spanish and South
" American dollars shall constitute a legal tender, under
" Her Majesty's Proclamation and Orders in Council
" of the 4th March, 1844, has been adjusted with refe-
" rence to the intrinsic value of the coins of proper
" weight, as compared with the British sovereign, or
" pound sterling.

" In the case of silver coins, this comparative value
" could only be properly determined by reference, first,
" to the contents of the coins in pure silver; and se-
" condly, to the marketable value of that silver in British
" sterling money. This value, as indicated by the trans-
" actions in the principal bullion markets of the world
" for some years past, has been ascertained to be equiva-
" lent, as nearly as may be, to a money price of 5s.
" British sterling for the ounce of silver of British stand-
" ard fineness; and it is according to this price that the
" rates at which foreign silver coins should circulate, and
" be a legal tender in the British colonies, are to be de-
" termined.

" The silver coins of the United Kingdom, being, in
" effect, tokens passing at nominal rates above their
" intrinsic value, no reference can be had, in fixing the
" rates for which foreign coins shall circulate, to the
" quantity of silver they may contain, as compared with
" that actually contained in British coins.

" The circumstances under which British silver coins,
" and the silver coins of foreign states, can be procured
" for circulation in the colonies, are by no means analo-
" gous. To the coinage and issue of foreign coins there
" is no limitation; and they may, consequently, at all
" times be purchased, without limitation as to quan-
" tity, at a price according closely with their intrinsic
" worth.

" The British silver coins, on the contrary, are only to
" be procured in limited amount, by special orders for their
" preparation and issue at Her Majesty's Mint, and upon
" payment for them of their full nominal value ; and they
" are not to be obtained from the Mint upon application
" of any party who may casually require them ; and al-
" though these coins are, as above stated, strictly speak-
" ing, only tokens, and are a legal tender within the
" United Kingdom to a limited amount only, they are
" readily accepted in payment of sums much beyond that
" limit, and, in all ordinary pecuniary transactions, their
" nominal value is fully maintained.

" In the colonies, the value of these coins is further
" established and maintained, by their being made re-
" ceivable at their nominal rates, in payment of all public
" duties under either imperial or colonial laws, and in
" exchange for all bills negociated for the public service,
" and on all other public money transactions ; and by
" their being also generally available for remittance to
" the mother country, or to other colonies.

" In consideration of these circumstances, and of the
" ample security they afford for the realization, at all
" times, of the full nominal value of the coins, it has
" been found expedient that British silver coins, at their
" nominal value, should be a legal tender without limi-
" tation."

THE EXCHANGE WITH THE COLONIES.

Before proceeding to describe the metallic currency of the more distant colonies, it is desirable to advert to the fluctuations of the mercantile exchange between the colonies and Great Britain.

Although the commercial interchange between the colonies and the mother country is fettered by regulations from which the commerce of the latter with the rest of the world is, in a great measure, free, yet the laws which determine the relative value of their respective productions, and the course of the mercantile exchange between them, are the same in both cases. Export and import duties, and the confinement of the trade of the colonies to particular channels, may affect the money value of those productions, and the terms and conditions on which they are bartered for the commodities of other countries, but can have no permanent effect on the mercantile exchange, which, as is justly observed by Mr. Ricardo, " is never " ascertained by estimating the comparative value " of money in corn, cloth, or any other commodity, " but by estimating the value of currency of one " country in the currency of another."

It is not necessary, in order to determine this relation, that the currencies of the two countries should be composed of the same metal; the one may be gold and the other silver, and yet, at any given time, a correct estimate may be made of their comparative value. The currency of this country, for example, is based upon gold, that of France upon silver. It is wished to ascertan the value of the one relatively to that of the other. How is this question to be determined? There appears to be but one way of solving the problem; it is necessary for this purpose to ascertain the value of fine gold or of fine silver, in the respective terms of the currencies of the two countries; by this means a correct estimate of the relative value of the two currencies may be formed.

As an examination of the course of the mercantile exchange between England and France, and of the circumstances by which its variations are limited, may serve to illustrate the principle on which the operations of exchange depend, and with reference to which they are conducted, it may be useful to follow out that examination into some detail.

In France a kilogramme of gold, $\frac{9}{10}$ fine, is coined into 3100 francs, of which 6 francs are retained by the Mint for brassage.*

In England an ounce of gold, $\frac{11}{12}$ fine, is coined into 3*l*. 17*s*. 10½*d*. sterling.

$$1 \text{ kilogramme} = 15{,}436 \text{ grains.}$$
$$1 \text{ ounce} = 480 \text{ grains.}$$

* Ordinance of the king, Feb. 25, 1835.

The fine gold contained in 15·436 grains of French gold are 13·893 grains.

The fine gold contained in 480 grains of English gold are 440 grains.

If 13·893 grains of fine gold produce, at the French Mint, 3·094 francs, then 113·001 grains (the fine gold contained in a sovereign) will produce 25 francs 16½ centimes.

If 440 grains of fine gold produce, at the British Mint, 3l. 17s. 10½d., then 113·001 grains will produce 1l.

It thus appears that, according to the respective regulations of the Mints of England and France, one pound of English money is equal to 25 francs, 16½ centimes, of French money.

But silver being rated, at the French Mint, higher in proportion to gold than the proportion that generally obtains in the commercial world, the latter metal commonly bears a premium, as against silver, varying from about 5 to about 15 per mille, that is to say, a given amount of francs, in gold coin, is worth more than the same amount of francs, in silver coin.

Suppose that premium at any given time to be 10 per mille, then, at that time, 25·41½ francs, and not 25·16½ francs, (as deduced from the Mint regulations,) of French money, will be of the same value as 1l. of English money.

The actual course of exchange between England and France cannot materially differ from the computed par to a greater extent than is sufficient to cover the expense of transmitting gold, or silver, from London to Paris, or Paris to London.

Suppose that expense to be the half of 1 per cent.; the actual course of exchange may, in that case, diverge from the computed par to a corresponding extent: it may rise to 25·54, or fall to 25·29 francs, per pound sterling, for bills payable at sight.

This rise or fall would be the extent of the divergence from the computed par, on the supposition above-stated, if there were no other circumstances to affect it.

But there are other considerations to be taken into account.

Although no charge is made at the British Mint for seignorage or brassage, yet 125·551 grains of French gold (equal to 113·001 grains of fine gold) cannot be converted into a sovereign, without previously incurring some expense.

1st. There is a delay of about a fortnight in effecting the coinage; hence, the price of standard gold in London is not 3*l.* 17*s.* 10½*d.* per ounce, but only 3*l.* 17*s.* 9*d.* per ounce; the difference of 1½*d.* per ounce being a compensation for the loss of interest.

2nd. Although a pound, troy weight, of standard gold is coined into 46*l.* 14*s.* 6*d.*, yet a quantity of foreign gold, in coin or in bars, containing the same quantity of fine gold as is contained in

46*l*. 14*s*. 6*d*. of English gold coin, is not worth 46*l*. 14*s*. 6*d*. in English money; for, before the foreign gold can be sold as standard gold, certain expenses will have to be incurred, which must be borne by the seller.

On an ingot of 15 lb., those expenses are as follows :—

			s.	*d.*
Melting	.	.	4	0
Assay	.	.	5	0
Waste	.	.	6	0

which sum of fifteen shillings, apportioned on 15 lb. weight, is equal to one penny per ounce.

Besides this expense of one penny per ounce, there will be a loss of one-eighth of a carat grain, in the assay; for as no notice is taken, in the assayer's report, of anything less than ⅛th of a carat grain, in the fineness of gold, it follows, that if a bar of gold be $\frac{1}{16}$th or $\frac{1}{32}$nd of a carat grain worse than standard, it is reported to to be ⅛th of a grain worse.

The value of ⅛th of a carat grain is computed as follows :—

$$22 \text{ carats} = 88 \text{ carat grains.}$$

As 88 carat grains are to ⅛th of a carat grain, so are 480 troy grains to $\frac{1}{12}$ of a troy grain.

As 480 troy grains are to 3*l*. 17*s*. 9*d*., so are $\frac{1}{12}$ of a troy grain to one penny and $\frac{32}{100}$ of a penny.

This loss of 1⅓*d*. in the assay, added to the expense of 1*d*. for melting, &c., makes 2⅓*d*., which is the difference between the value of an ounce of standard gold and an ounce of foreign gold reduced, by calculation, to standard—of which foreign gold, the fineness has not been duly ascertained by assay.

It thus appears, that the aggregate amount of the expenses incurred by the importer of foreign gold, before that gold can be disposed of as standard gold, and the loss of interest, is $3\frac{5}{6}d.$ on $3l.$ $17s.$ $10\frac{1}{2}d.$, or $\frac{4}{10}$ of 1 per cent,—which expenses, together with the cost of transmission (supposed to be the half of 1 per cent.), being added to the computed par of $25\cdot41\frac{1}{2}$ francs, create an exchange of $25\cdot64$, at which rates, bills, payable at sight, or the transmission of gold from Paris to London, are equally advantageous to the remitter.

Presuming that the same charges are incurred in the sale of gold at Paris as in London, namely, the loss of a fortnight's interest, and the expense of melting and assay, amounting together to $\frac{4}{10}$ of 1 per cent., the exchange might fall from the computed par of $25\cdot41\frac{1}{2}$ to $25\cdot19$, at which rate bills payable at sight, or the transmission of gold from London to Paris, would be an equally advantageous remittance.

Thus far the course of exchange between London and Paris, and the natural limit to its variations, have been considered with reference to the expenses attending the transmission and sale of *gold*.

It may be useful to consider in what way, and to what extent, the variations of the exchange are controlled and limited by the transmission of *silver*.

In England, there is no Mint price of silver. In the purchase and sale of silver in the market, however, the old Mint standard of fineness, namely, 11 ozs. 2 dwts. ($\frac{222}{240}$), is still adhered to, that is to say, a bar of silver of which the fineness has been ascertained by assay, is reduced, by calculation, to the standard of 11 ozs. 2 dwts., and sold at the market price of silver of that standard.

In France, the Mint is open to the public for the coinage of both metals.

A kilogramme of silver, $\frac{9}{10}$ fine, is coined into 200 francs, of which 2 francs are retained by the Mint for brassage;* and as, for a kilogramme of gold of the same fineness, there are delivered from the Mint 3094 francs in gold coin, the proportionate value of fine silver to fine gold is estimated at the Mint as 15·62 to 1.

If this proportionate value prevailed in the London market, the price of standard silver in London would be $60\frac{27}{100}$ pence per ounce; for as the market price of *standard* gold is 933 pence (3*l.* 17*s.* 9*d.*) per ounce, the price of *fine* gold must be $1017\frac{8}{10}$ pence (4*l.* 4*s.* $9\frac{8}{10}d.$) per ounce. The latter sum, divided by 15·62, gives $65\frac{16}{100}$ pence as the price of *fine* silver, or $60\frac{27}{100}$ pence per ounce as the price of standard silver.

In the general market of the commercial world,

* Ordinance of the king, Feb. 25, 1835.

the value of silver relatively to gold may be taken, on an average, to be as 15·73 to 1.

According to this proportion, the premium on gold, at Paris, should be $6\frac{6}{10}$ per mille, and the price of standard silver in London, $59\frac{7}{10}$ pence per ounce.

When the premium on gold at Paris is $6\frac{6}{10}$ per mille, the computed par of exchange with London, gold against gold, is 25 francs 33 centimes per pound sterling.

When the price of standard silver, in London, is $59\frac{7}{10}$ pence per ounce, the computed par of exchange, silver against silver, is likewise 25 francs 33 centimes per pound sterling.

This would be the computed par of exchange, if the value of silver compared with gold, in London and at Paris, were constantly and uniformly as 15·73 to 1.

But the value of the two metals, relatively to each other, is continually varying, and is especially affected by every alteration in the course of exchange between London and Paris. When the exchange is so far in favour of London as to induce an importation of gold, the demand for gold at Paris naturally raises the premium on that metal. The same cause naturally lowers the price of silver in London. Indeed, in consequence of the large and continued influx of silver from Mexico and South America, the value of silver, in relation to gold, is generally so much lower in London than at Paris, as to allow of its exportation, whatever may be the state of the exchanges. More silver is imported from the countries which are in possession of the mines, than is required for the use and consumption of this country. The excess is naturally exported.

The object of the foregoing observations on the exchange between England and France, and the natural limit to its variations, is to show that, in order to ascertain the extent of that limit, it is necessary to take into consideration, not only the expense of transmitting the precious metals from one place to another, but likewise all the direct and indirect expense and loss of time required for the conversion (either directly or through the purchase and sale of bullion) of the money of one country into the money of another.

In the operations of exchange between the principal commercial towns of Europe, a very small excess over the natural limit, that is to say, a very small profit—perhaps $\frac{1}{4}$ of 1 per cent.—is sufficient to induce the movement of gold and silver from one country to another. And,—such are the shrewdness and competition among those engaged in operations of this nature,—however large may be the balance of payments to be effected, or however forcible the current—that limit, or that profit, would not be materially exceeded.

Not so in the exchange between Great Britain and her colonies; neither the same sharp-sighted competition, nor the same facility of computing, beforehand, the precise result of a direct or circuitous operation in the business of exchange, are found in the colonies as in London, and the principal marts of Europe.

It may be observed, moreover, that in London, Paris, Hamburgh, and other places, dealings in foreign bills of exchange are commonly undertaken, not merely as subsidiary and subordinate to other business, but as a *principal* source of profit. That profit is indeed small on each particular transaction, but it is nearly certain, and, when derived from a large amount of business, becomes important.

In the colonies, this branch of business is, in a great measure, subsidiary and subordinate ; and as the field of its operations is comparatively narrow, the variations of the exchange from the computed par is occasionally considerable. The natural limit to those variations depends, indeed, on the same principle as that which governs the variations of the exchange between London and Paris, but, from the causes above mentioned, that limit, in the colonies, is of wider range.

It is here necessary to advert to a circumstance which, although its nature and consequences are sufficiently obvious, has sometimes been the occasion of misapprehension and mistake—namely, the difference in the rates of exchange at which bills are negotiated in England upon other places, and at those other places upon England.

This difference in the case of the more distant colonies is sometimes considerable.

The case of the Australian colonies will serve as an example.

Under ordinary circumstances, no person will give more English money in London, for a given amount of money, payable at Sydney, than the English money, if sent thither, will produce, after paying the cost of carriage, insurance, &c.

The freight, insurance, and charges of the shipment and conveyance of specie from London to New South Wales may be estimated at 3 per cent.

The exchange on a bill drawn in London on New South Wales, and payable at sight, cannot therefore, under ordinary circumstances, exceed 103l. for 100l.

When the exchange, London on New South Wales, is 103l. for 100l., the exchange, New South Wales on London, will be 94$\frac{1}{3}l$. for a bill for 100l. on London, or which is the same thing, 100l. will be given in New South Wales for a bill for 106l. on London; for whether a merchant in London purchases a bill for 100l. for 103l., and remits the bill to New South Wales, or instructs his correspondent there to draw upon him at sight for 106l., comes to the same thing, the difference in the exchange being compensated by the gain of interest for the time (supposed to be seven months) during which the payment in London is postponed.

On the other hand, no person, under ordinary

circumstances, will give more money at Sydney for a given sum of money payable in London, than the Sydney money if sent to London will produce there, after paying the cost of carriage, &c.

The exchange on a bill drawn at Sydney upon London, and payable at sight for 100*l.*, cannot therefore, under ordinary circumstances, exceed 103*l.*

When the exchange, New South Wales upon London, is 103*l.* in New South Wales for a bill of 100*l.* on London, the exchange, London on New South Wales, will be 100*l.* in London for a bill for 106*l.* on New South Wales.

In short, the conditions described in the last-mentioned case will be reversed.

It may be useful to point out the difference of exchange in the more complicated case of London on Bengal, and Bengal upon London.

The metallic money of Bengal consists of the rupees of the East India Company. A rupee contains 165 grains of fine silver and 15 grains of alloy. Assuming that 444 grains of fine silver (the fine silver contained in an ounce of standard silver) are worth five shillings per ounce, then 165 grains of fine silver are worth 1*s.* 10·297*d.*

The charge to the public for coinage, at the Bengal Mint, is 2 per cent. The computed par of exchange between London and Bengal is, therefore, 1*s.* 10·743*d.*

The cost of sending 165 grains of fine silver to

Bengal, and converting that silver into a rupee, will be as follows:—

	d.
Value of 165 grains of fine silver, in London	22·297
Mint charge 2 per cent.	·446
Freight, insurance, &c., 3 per cent. . .	·669
	23·412

Now, suppose that to convey silver from London to Bengal, and to coin that silver into rupees, require a period of four months, and that the transmission of a bill of exchange to Bengal, payable sixty days after sight, and its realization there, require the same period of time, then the purchase of a bill on Bengal, at an exchange of $1s.$ $11·412d.$ per rupee, payable sixty days after sight, or the transmission of specie, are to the transmitter the same thing.

At Bengal, bills upon London are commonly drawn at ten months' date.

When the exchange, London on Bengal, for bills at sixty days' sight is $1s.$ 11 $412d.$ per rupee, the exchange, Bengal upon London, for a bill at ten months' date should be $2s.$ $0·777d.$ per rupee;* for, whether a merchant buys a bill upon Bengal at sixty days' sight at an exchange of $1s.$ $11·412d.$ per rupee, sends silver to Bengal to be coined into rupees, or directs his correspondent in India to

---

	d.
* Bill at 60 days' sight realized at Calcutta in four months	23·412
14 months' interest at 5 per cent.	1·365
	24·777

draw upon him a bill at ten months' date at the exchange of 2s. 0·777d. per rupee, comes to the same thing, the difference in the exchange being compensated by the gain of interest.

The value of a rupee in London (assuming the price of standard silver to be five shillings per ounce) is—

	d.
	22·297
The freight, insurance, &c. from Bengal to London may be taken at 3 per cent. .	·668
	21·629

If the value of the rupee be realized in London in four months from the date of its shipment at Bengal, and if a bill drawn at Bengal upon London at sixty days' sight can be realized in the same time, then the exchange, Bengal upon London, for a bill at sixty days' sight, should be 1s. 9·629d. per rupee.

When the exchange, Bengal upon London, for a bill at sixty days' sight is 1s. 9·629d. per rupee, the exchange for a bill at ten months' date should be 1s. 10·169d. per rupee.

The exchange, London on Bengal, in the last-mentioned case, for a bill at sixty days' sight, should be 1s. 8·876d.

It thus appears that the exchange, London on Bengal, for bills at sixty days' sight, may rise to 1s. 11·412d., or 3 per cent. above the computed par of 1s. 10·743d., or fall to 1s. 8·876d., or 8 $\frac{2}{10}$ per cent. below the computed par; and that the exchange, Bengal upon London, for bills at ten months' date, may rise to 2s. 0·777d., or 9 per cent. above the computed par, or fall to 1s. 10·169d., or 3 per cent. below the computed par, without being checked by the transmission of specie.

No allowance is made in the foregoing cases for the charge of agency, nor for the risk of dishonour to, and the non-payment of, bills.* These considerations, and the risk of fluctuations in the exchange during the long period of time which is required to complete a transaction of this nature, between countries so distant from each other as England and India, frequently render the variations of the exchange much greater than are indicated in the imaginary cases above stated.

* Bills drawn by the officers of the Commissariat on the Lords of the Treasury, in consequence of their superior credit, are generally negotiated at an exchange more favourable to the seller of the bills—especially in the more distant colonies—than the bills of private merchants.

When the state of the mercantile exchange in any of the colonies, with England, is unfavourable to the negotiations of the Commissariat Officer, that is, when the exchange is said to be " against " England, those negotiations are supported by the transmission to him of specie, and are seldom effected at a lower rate than the computed par. Those negotiations are generally conducted with great judgment and discretion.

THE WESTERN COAST OF AFRICA.

In the British colonies on the western coast of Africa, the British denominations of pounds, shillings, and pence, are used in commercial dealings.

In the year 1843, it was ordained by an Order of Her Majesty in Council, and by a proclamation issued for that purpose, that in the British colonies and possessions at Sierra Leone, Cape Coast, and elsewhere, on the western coast of Africa, the doubloon and dollar of Spain, Mexico, and South America, the French gold piece of 20 francs, and the French piece of 5 francs, shall circulate and be received in payment at the following rates, that is to say :—

	s.	d.
The doubloon at the rate of	64	0
The dollar at the rate of	4	2
The 20-franc piece at the rate of . .	15	10
The 5-franc piece at the rate of . . .	3	10½

And that in all payments, to be made in the said colonies and possessions, tender of payment in the said coins, at the respective rates above mentioned, shall be deemed and taken to be a lawful tender, in the same manner as if such tender had been made in the current coin of the United Kingdom.

Previously to the last-mentioned period, the silver dollar of Spain, Mexico, and South America, circulated and was received in payment, in accordance with the Order in Council of the 25th

March, 1825, at the rate of 4s. 4d.; and as a doubloon was deemed equal to 16 dollars, the rate at which that coin circulated was 69s. 4d.

At these respective rates, the concurrent circulation of the two coins, in a sound and perfect state, was impossible. Doubloons accumulated in the hands of merchants, and in the colonial treasury ; while silver dollars, when occasionally put into circulation by the officers of the Commissariat, or otherwise, were collected and exported. British coins of gold and silver were likewise, in consequence of being undervalued 4 per cent. with reference to the dollar, and 8 per cent. with reference to the doubloon, excluded from the circulation.

A mistaken notion of the causes which rendered the retention of silver dollars in circulation impracticable, led to the injurious device of cutting or otherwise mutilating those coins, in the expectation that a diminution of their value would lessen the inducement to export them.

This mischievous practice had the effect of exposing the Government of Sierra Leone to the inconvenience and expense of ultimately calling in and redeeming them.

In a report from the Lieut.-Governor of the British settlements on the Gold Coast to the Secretary of State for the Colonies, it is stated that gold dust is the principal currency of that colony, and that all payments are made in it ; that the coins in circulation are British gold, silver, and copper coins, Spanish and South American dollars, and a few French 5-franc pieces.

It is further stated that, as the principal commercial currency of the colony is gold dust, valued at 4l. per ounce, and that, as the produce of an ounce of gold dust, when transmitted to England, after deducting freight, insurance, commission, &c., is, on an average, 3l. 12s. per ounce, the exchange (the par of exchange) is generally quoted at 11¼ for bills on England, at three days' sight; that is to say, a bill upon England for 90l. will purchase 25 ounces of gold dust, equal to 100l. currency.

The amount of the coins in this settlement, in the year 1847, is estimated by the Lieut.-Governor to have been as follows :—

	£.
British coins	1500
Spanish and South American dollars . .	200
Coins of other countries	200

In a similar communication from the Governor of the British settlement on the Gambia, it is stated that, in that colony, merchants' accounts are kept in pounds, shillings, and pence sterling; also in pounds, shillings, and pence currency, calculating four dollars to the pound, or five shillings to the dollar, and in proportion for the lesser coins; and also in dollars and cents, some houses adopting one method and some the other.

The use of gold dust as the medium of interchange at the Gold Coast, and of what are called

currency denominations at the Gambia, can be regarded only as conventional. Those denominations and media are readily convertible, by an easy
arithmetical process, into sterling money, with
reference to which all contracts and engagements,
whether expressed in currency denominations, or
in dollars and cents, or for the payment of gold
dust, must be construed and determined.

A notion appears to have occasionally prevailed
in these settlements, as well as in other of the
British colonies, that it is politic and desirable to
prevent, by artificial means and contrivances, the
free exportation of gold and silver coins, and to
retain them for the purposes of domestic circulation.

Those who entertained this notion appear to
have overlooked the consideration that if it were
possible, by laws which could not be evaded, or
by any other means, to effect this purpose, the consequence would be an unfavourable exchange with
other countries, and an enhancement of the nominal prices of all domestic produce, and of all imported commodities. The purchasing power of a
given amount of the coins so artificially pent up
would be lessened, and all pay and incomes of a
certain nominal amount would be diminished in
value.

Suggestions of this nature have been wisely and
properly disregarded by Her Majesty's Government. By the Order in Council and royal procla-

mation of the 10th June, 1843, the metallic money of those settlements has been placed under just and salutary regulation. A considerable proportion of the doubloons which, in consequence of the high nominal rates formerly assigned to them, relatively to the rates assigned to other coins, had inconveniently accumulated at Sierra Leone and the Gambia, will, it is probable, be exported; but their place will be gradually supplied, through the natural stream of commerce, and by the operations of the Commissariat, with other coins more suitably adapted to the local circulation.

CURRENCY OF ST. HELENA AND THE CAPE OF GOOD HOPE.

1. *Saint Helena.*

It appears, by a Despatch from the Court of Directors of the East India Company to the Governor and Council of St. Helena, dated the 21st July, 1819, that the coins, which at that time were authorized to pass current in the island, were respectively rated as follows :—

	£.	s.	d.
Star Pagoda	0	7	6
Gold Mohur	1	12	8
Doubloon	3	13	6
French Napoleon	0	16	10
Venetian	0	9	2
Spanish Dollar—German Crown .	0	4	8
Rupee (Sicca)	0	2	1
Denatoon	0	5	7
French Crown	0	4	2
Porto Novo	0	6	3

It further appears, that although the coins above mentioned were issued in payments to the troops and civil functionaries of the island at the rates respectively assigned to them, yet the same coins were received into the Treasury in payment for articles supplied from the public stores, at rates about 7 per cent. higher than those at which they were issued.

This difference in the value of the coins, between their issue and receipt, appears to have been adopted with the view and in the hope of keeping the coined money in the island.

Thus expectation of confining its metallic currency to the circulation of the island probably originated in the notion—at that time not uncommon —that the movement of coins of gold and silver may be artificially restrained and regulated by an arbitrary alteration of the rates and denominations by which those coins are designated.

This erroneous notion was probably strengthened in the minds of those who entertained it, by the consideration, that, as the island of St. Helena produces no exportable commodities, and as the stores, &c. required for its consumption were supplied, in kind, chiefly by the East India Company, the frequent importation and exportation of the precious metals might be prevented and rendered unnecessary, by giving to the coins which constituted the domestic currency of the island what was vainly imagined to be a higher value than they bore in other countries.

Experience demonstrated the fallacy of this notion. In the Despatch above referred to, it is observed that the object of keeping the currency in the island had failed, as the situation of the island, in this respect, at the date of the Despatch, sufficiently proved.

With a view of affording relief to the deficiency in the metallic currency of the island, at that time complained of, the Court of Directors ordered the transmission to St. Helena of 50,000*l.*, in dollars.

Soon after the transference of the government of St. Helena from the East India Company to the Crown, that is to say, in the year 1836, the Governor of St. Helena issued a proclamation declaring the rates, in sterling money, at which the foreign gold and silver coins therein specified shall pass current in the island.

Those rates were as follows :—

	£.	s.	d.
Doubloon	3	6	0
Star Pagoda	0	7	3
Louis-d'or and Napoleon . . .	0	15	7
Dollar, Spanish and American . .	0	4	4
Bombay rupee	0	1	11
Five-franc piece	0	4	0
Two-franc piece	0	1	8
One-franc piece	0	0	10

The rates, in sterling money, thus assigned to the foreign coins, authorized in this proclamation to pass current in the island, were too high to admit the concurrent circulation of British gold and silver coins; hence, the currency of the island consisted principally of Spanish and American dollars, and other foreign coins of gold and silver.

On the 15th July, 1843, Her Majesty in Council ordered a proclamation to be issued, declaring that throughout the island of St. Helena the gold doubloon of Spain, Mexico, and South America shall circulate and be received as being of the full value of 64s. sterling, and that the silver dollar of Spain, Mexico, and the South American States shall circulate, and be received in payment as being of the full value of 4s. 2d. sterling.

A notification was, at the same time, published by the Governor of the island, intimating, that on certain days mentioned in the notification, the officer in charge of the Commissariat would receive such coins as were excluded by Her Majesty's proclamation from the circulation of the colony, at the rates at which they had been previously current, and would give in exchange for them such money as is made current by that proclamation, or bills on the Lords Commissioners of the Treasury.

The various coins brought to the officer in charge of the Commissariat in consequence of this notification, amounting to 11,748l. 7s. 8½d., were transmitted to England, melted, and sold as bullion.

The currency of this island is now placed on a sound and satisfactory foundation. No conflicting coins nor conflicting money denominations will, in future, induce the necessity of large and frequent importations and exportations of specie; and it may reasonably be expected that the Government and the Commissariat chests will be regularly supplied with money, through the negotiation of bills in England, without occasioning any material disturbance to the domestic circulation of the colony.

2. *Cape of Good Hope.*

From the period of its first capture by the
British forces in the year 1795, until the year
1826, this colony experienced all the uncertainty
and disadvantage of an inconvertible paper currency.

The paper rix-dollar of the Cape was first issued
by the Dutch East India Company in the year
1781, and was declared to be equal to 48 full-
weighted pennies of Holland, nearly equal to four
shillings of the sterling money of Great Britain.

At the period of the first British capture of the
colony in 1795, the amount of paper in circulation
was 1,291,276 rix dollars, of which sum, 611,276
rix-dollars consisted of the balance of the issues
and repayments of the sums disbursed for the public service, and 680,000 advanced to the public on
mortgage, through the medium of the Government Bank.

On the surrender of the colony to the British
forces in 1795, it was stipulated in the 8th Article
of the capitulation, that His Britannic Majesty
should establish the value of the paper currency;
and the Colonial Government engaged to represent
to His Majesty's Government the expediency of
adopting such arrangements as might appear necessary to establish its credit, or, if possible, entirely
to liquidate it.

Whatever might have been the understanding or
the stipulations entered into upon that occasion, a

large addition appears to have been made to the paper circulation, by the British Government, during the eight years from the capture of the colony in 1795, to its restoration to the Dutch, in 1803. The effect of that increase was a depreciation of the value of the currency, of 20 to 30 per cent., as compared with the value of 48 full-weighted pennies of Holland.

Although, on the restoration of the colony to the Dutch in 1803, a full equivalent for such part of the paper currency as had been issued for the purposes of the British Government, was paid in military and naval stores, no reduction was subsequently made by the Dutch Government in its amount; on the contrary, the existing paper money was called in, and an issue of fresh notes was made, amounting to about 2,000,000 rix dollars

During the period of the Dutch occupation, bills on Holland were negotiated at a premium of 160; reducing the value of the paper rix dollars to nearly 1s. 6d. sterling, and the value of a Spanish dollar to 2½ or 3 paper rix dollars.

After the surrender of the colony to the British forces in 1806, that is, between the years 1810 and 1814, a further issue of 1,000,000 rix dollars was effected through the medium of the Government Bank. The value of the paper gradually sank until the year 1825, when it reached its lowest point of depression, namely, 1s. 5d.

On the 6th June, 1825, an ordinance was published by the Governor in Council, stating, that " His Majesty's Government had determined to " establish the British currency as the circulating " medium in all the colonial possessions of the " Crown; and had further been pleased to order and " direct that the British silver money shall be a " legal tender, in this colony, at the rate of 1s. 6d. " for each rix dollar, and so in proportion for any " greater or less sum ;" and ordering that, from the 1st January, 1826, all public accounts shall be kept, and all contracts made for the public service, in pounds, shillings, and pence.

Some years before the publication of this ordinance, a controversy had arisen in the colony, as to the nature and extent of the depreciation of the paper rix dollar. On one hand it was contended, that the value of the paper, as compared with specie, had not arisen from an excessive issue; and that the premium on the exchange with England was produced by excessive importation, and by a balance of payments continually accumulating, adverse to the colony.

On the other hand, it was said that the value of a paper currency, with reference to gold and silver, depends on the quantity of business which it has to perform in the country where it circulates, and should be proportionable to the quantity of the objects of property which require to be circulated; that the high nominal price of Spanish dollars, and the inordinate premium on the exchange with England and Holland, were themselves, a sufficient proof of an excessive issue ; and that it was incumbent on the issuers to contract the amount of paper in circulation, until its value was restored to its original level.

These conflicting opinions were the perpetual source of adverse discussion; and it was to be expected that, when the above-mentioned ordinance was first promulgated, there would arise, in the minds of many of the inhabitants of the colony, feelings of dissatisfaction and discontent.

Those who thought that 4s. of British money (equivalent to a metallic rix dollar of Holland), ought to have been fixed for the redemption of the paper rix dollar, were principally landed proprietors and capitalists. It is doubtful, however, whether this class of persons would have derived any real or ultimate advantages from such an arrangement. The nominal value of their property would have been lessened by it, while the real value of the mortgages upon that property, and of their debts, would have been greatly increased. Besides, as the debt created by the issue of paper money, was contracted for colonial purposes, the colony must have borne the cost and expenses of its redemption; and the landed proprietors would have had to sustain a large portion of the taxes which such an arrangement would have rendered necessary.

With respect to the other classes of the community, it may be observed, that, as the sums due to the Colonial Government in paper money, through the Lombard Bank, constituted a very large proportion of the whole amount in circulation, the debtors of those sums would have been injured rather than benefited by an enhancement of its value.

In fixing the average rate at which bills on England had been negotiated at the Cape, for several years previous to 1825, namely, 1s. 6d. for a rix dollar, no interference in the relations of debtor and creditor in any recent debts and engagements, was used, nor was any difficulty or inconvenience in the ordinary transactions of buying and selling in the colony, occasioned.

If there existed any special case in which the holders of paper could make out a legal or equitable title to have their paper discharged by the Government at the rate of 4s. sterling per rix dollar, it was open to such parties to state, and establish the peculiar circumstances and considerations on which their claim was founded.

In the year 1835, the outstanding rix dollar paper was, by order of the Government, made payable or exchangeable only at the Treasury. As the amount presented for payment was inconsiderable, it was notified to the public by proclamation, in the year 1840, that no rix dollar notes would be paid or exchanged after the 31st March, 1841, when all accounts relating to those notes would be finally closed.

The liquidation of the paper rix dollar currency was, in this way, finally accomplished.

Conformable to the ordinance of the 1st January, 1826, the public accounts are kept in sterling money; but among private persons, the old mode of reckoning in rix dollars, skillings, and stivers, is still practised; and biddings at sales of goods by auction, are made in these denominations.

Fixed property is sold by auction, in guilders, each of which is equal to sixpence sterling.

The value and rates of rix dollars, &c., in British money, are as follows:—

	£.	s.	d.
1 stiver	0	0	$0\frac{3}{8}$
6 stivers = 1 skilling . . .	0	0	$2\frac{1}{4}$
1 rix dollar = 8 skillings . .	0	1	6

The coins now in circulation, consist of sovereigns and half-sovereigns, and of British silver and copper coins. Foreign coins, consisting chiefly of Spanish, Mexican, and South American dollars, and of rupees, occasionally appear in the colony, but are not used as the medium of circulation.

The paper circulation of the colony at present consists of notes of five pounds and upwards, issued by three private banking establishments, the aggregate amount of which notes, it is supposed, does not, on the average, exceed 30,000*l.*

CURRENCY OF MAURITIUS.

The public accounts of this island, since the 1st January, 1826, have been kept in sterling money.

Merchants, bankers, and shopkeepers, in their ordinary dealings, reckon, and keep their accounts, either in dollars and centimes, or in dollars, livres, and sous.

1 dollar = 100 centimes
1 dollar = 10 livres
1 livre = 20 sous.

The dollar, the centime, the livre, and the sous, are merely denominations, or money of account.

Soon after the Order in Council of the 23rd March, 1825, was received at the Mauritius, it was declared by an ordinance of the Governor and Council of the island, that certain foreign coins shall be received and paid at the public offices, at the rates specified in the ordinance.

Those rates were as follows:—

	Gross Weight.	Pure Contents.	Value in Standard Silver.		To be paid to the Troops.	
	grs.	grs.	s.	d.	s.	d.
FRENCH.						
Piece of 5 francs	385	349·9	4	0·16	4	0
Piece of 2 francs	155	138·8	1	7·38	1	8
Piece of 1 franc	77½	69·4	0	9·69	0	10
SICILIAN.						
Dollar or scudi	422	382·2	4	0·62	4	1
Piece of 40 grains	141	117·5	·1	4·40	1	5
Piece of 20 grains	72	59·1	0	8·25	0	9
SPANISH.						
Dollar	416	370·9	4	3·79	4	4
UNITED STATES.						
Dollar	416	370·1	4	3·68	4	4
EAST INDIES.						
Calcutta rupee	192	175·9	2	0·56	2	1
Bombay or Surat rupee . .	179	164·7	1	11·10	1	11
Nominal dollar of the Mauritius	..	..	4	0	..	

As, by the ordinance, the value of the Mauritius dollar of account was fixed at 4s. sterling money of the United Kingdom,* and as the rates at which coins were received at the public offices, determined the rate at which they were received and paid in the ordinary dealings of the colony, all contracts and engagements entered into subsequently to the 1st January, 1826, and expressed in terms of the dollar of Mauritius and its sub-divisions, were contracts and engagements for the payment of sterling money, or its equivalent in foreign coins.

The gross weights, and contents in pure silver, of the coins specified in the above-mentioned ordinance, are the same as those contained in a table published by the late Dr. Kelly, and are said to be the results of assays made at the mints of London and Paris.

Notwithstanding this authority, the accuracy of the weights and fineness of the several coins above specified, is, at least, questionable.

In Dr. Kelly's table it is stated that the pure contents of a Spanish dollar are $370\frac{9}{10}$ grains ; and

---

* The words of the Ordinance are as follows:—" His Excellency " the Governor in Council, in conformity to the instructions and prin- " ciples laid down by Her Majesty for the guidance of the Local Govern- " ment, is further pleased to notify and declare that a tender and payment " of four shillings British silver money, or British silver and copper money, " shall, in this colony and its dependencies, be considered equivalent to, " and a legal tender and payment of, one current dollar of Mauritius, " under whatsoever denomination the same may have been known or " received—the said dollar being of the value of ten livres—without pre- " judice, however, to the interest of parties in those cases in which Spanish " dollars shall have been stipulated for as the *specific coin* in which pay- " ment was to be made."

that its value at 5s. 2d. per ounce of silver of the British standard, is 4s. $3\frac{70}{100}d$.

By later assays at the British mint, it appears that the pure contents of a Spanish, Mexican, or South American dollar, are on an average, 373 grains, of which the value, at 5s. 2d. per ounce of standard silver, is 4s. 4·07d.

In the table, the pure silver contained in a five-franc piece is stated to be 344·9 grains, and of a one-franc piece 69·4 grains.

According to the regulations of the French mint, the pure contents of a five-franc piece should be 347·30 grains, of a two-franc piece 138·92 grains, and of a one-franc piece 69·46 grains.

If the table in the Mauritius ordinance had been accurately constructed, the value of a five-franc piece would have been stated to be 4s. 0·50d., and the value of a one-franc piece to be 9·70d.; and if, in order to avoid inconvenient fractions, the five-franc piece had been received and paid at the public offices, at the rate of 4s., the value assigned to the two and one-franc pieces would probably have been 1s. 7d. and $9\frac{1}{2}d$. respectively, or about one per cent. below their value, relatively to the five-franc piece at 4s. Having been rated at 1s. 8d. and 10d. respectively, they were over-rated, with reference to the five-franc piece, rather more than four per cent.

This over-valuation of one and two-franc pieces led to a large importation of those coins into the colony, the effect of which was the expulsion of other coins from circulation.

In a letter from the President of the Mauritius Bank to the Colonial Secretary, dated the 28th February, 1838, he says—"The French one and "two-franc pieces alone offered the importer a " profit ; and, accordingly, considerable sums have " been introduced, and they now constitute nearly " two-thirds of the money in daily circulation."

With a view to affording a remedy to this inconvenience, an ordinance was passed by the Government of Mauritius, in which ordinance it is stated that "serious inconvenience is felt from the ex- " tensive importation of one and two-franc coins " of France, which, under ordinance No. 3 of " 1825, are received and paid at the public offices, " at rates considerably exceeding their intrinsic " value, and the proportion they bear to the five- " franc and twenty-franc pieces of France ; that by " the value at which coins are received at the pub- " lic offices, the rate at which they circulate among " individuals is usually regulated in this colony ; " that from the enhanced value given to the one " and two-franc coins of France, many persons re- " fuse to receive them in payment, and the course " of business, and mercantile operations generally, " are greatly impeded and prejudiced thereby ; " that it has been represented to His Excellency " the Governor, that a remedy is urgently and im- " mediately required for the evil ; and that such

" remedy would be effectually obtained by reducing
" the rates at which the one and two-franc coins of
" France are received at the public offices, to that
" of their intrinsic value."

The ordinance then directs, that " from and after
" the publication of the ordinance, the one and two-
" franc coins of France shall be received and paid
" at the public offices, at the rate of five one-franc
" pieces for 4s., and of five two-franc pieces for 8s. ;
" nevertheless, the said pieces cannot be received
" in sums of less than 4s."

This ordinance would have effectually removed
the difficulty, if the two chartered banks of the
colony had adopted and faithfully observed its provisions ; but there is reason to suppose that those
institutions continued to issue the coins in question,
in discharge of their notes and liabilities, at the
rates which had previously been assigned to them,
that is to say, the one-franc piece at 10d., and the
two-franc piece at 1s. 8d., those rates being pro-
portionably higher than the rates assigned by the
ordinance of the 25th November, 1825, to the
Spanish dollar and the East India Company's
rupee.

If the provisions of the last-mentioned ordinance had been duly observed, the dollar, the East
India Company's rupee, and the coins of France,
being, within a very small fraction, correctly rated
relatively to each other in the ordinance of the
25th November, 1825, would, in all probability,

have formed the principal metallic circulation of the island, to the exclusion of the gold and silver coins of Great Britain.

In order to establish the concurrent circulation of British coins, the only consistent measure that could have been adopted, would have been the reduction of the rates of the foreign coins specified in the ordinance to their sterling value.

In this respect the case of the Mauritius differed from that of the West Indies and North America in a material point, which it is here proper to notice.

By the ordinance of November, 1825, the Mauritius dollar of account, in terms of which contracts of debt in that colony are commonly expressed, was fixed at 4s. of the money of Great Britain. An engagement, at the Mauritius, to pay 13 dollars was, therefore, an engagement to pay 2l. 12s. sterling ; which debt of 2l. 12s. might be discharged either with 2l. 12s. of British gold and silver coins, or with 12 silver dollars, or with certain other foreign coins at the rates legally assigned to them.

This was not the case in other colonies. His Majesty's Order in Council of the 23rd March, 1825, did not define the value of a given amount of the nominal currency of any of the colonies, but only ordained, that in all the colonial possessions of the Crown, the tender or payment of 4s. 4d. of English money shall be deemed equivalent to the tender or payment of a dollar. An engagement at Nova Scotia, for example, to pay 3*l.* in Halifax currency (in which currency the denomination of a dollar is 5*s.*), was not an engagement to pay 2*l.* 12*s.* in sterling money, or its equivalent, but to pay 12 dollars; which debt of 12 dollars might be legally discharged either with 12 silver dollars or with 2*l.* 12*s.* of British gold and silver.

In both cases, 12 silver dollars and 2*l.* 12*s.* in English money were equivalent tenders of payment; in both, 12 silver dollars were a cheaper tender of payment than 2*l.* 12*s.* in British coin. The difference between the two cases was this :— When it became necessary to correct the erroneous rates assigned under the authority of His Majesty's Order in Council of the 23rd March, 1825, the rectification had not the effect of requiring from a debtor at the Mauritius the payment of a greater or less amount of British gold and silver than before, but did require the payment of a greater number of dollars or other foreign coins than before; while, from the Halifax debtor, the same number of silver dollars, or other foreign coins, was required for the discharge of his debt as before, but a less amount of British gold and silver.

In short, the Mauritius debt was an engagement to pay a certain amount of *sterling money;* the Halifax debt was an engagement to pay a certain amount of *dollars.*

The correction of the erroneous rates assigned to foreign coins in the Mauritius ordinance of the 25th November, 1825,—erroneous with reference to British gold and silver coins—was effected by Her Majesty's Order in Council, and by proclamation dated February, 1843.

The rates assigned to foreign coins in that proclamation are as follows :—

The doubloon of Spain, Mexico, or the States of South America, at the rate of 64s. sterling.

The gold mohur of the East India Company's territory, coined since the 1st September, 1835, at the rate of 29s. 2d.

The French gold piece of 20 francs, at the rate of 15s. 10d.

The dollar of Spain, Mexico, and South America, at the rate of 4s. 2d.

The rupee of the East India Company's territory, coined since the 1st September, 1835, at the rate of 1s. 10d.

The French piece of five francs, or French pieces of one and two francs to the same amount (viz., five francs), at the rate of 3s. 10½d., provided that the said French silver coins shall not be a legal tender in sums of less than five francs.

The rates, in sterling money, assigned in this proclamation to foreign coins, when converted into the money of account of the Mauritius, that is to say, the nominal dollar and its divisions, give the following results :—

	Dollars.	Cents.
Doubloon	16	0
Gold mohur	7	$29\frac{1}{6}$
French 20-franc piece	3	$95\frac{5}{6}$
Spanish and Mexican dollar . . .	1	$4\frac{1}{6}$
Rupee	0	$45\frac{5}{6}$
Five-franc piece	0	$96\frac{21}{24}$

The rates fixed by Her Majesty's Proclamation, are not, however, practically adopted in the colony. Either from a desire to avoid the inconvenient fractions which result from the application of the rates fixed in Her Majesty's Proclamation, to the Mauritius dollar of account, or from some other motive, the merchants, bankers, traders, and others, of the Mauritius, in their dealings and transactions with each other, receive and pay the East India Company's rupee at the rate of two rupees to the Mauritius dollar; thus reducing the sterling value of that dollar, from 4s., as fixed in the Colonial Ordinance of the 25th November, 1825, to 3s. $8\frac{4}{10}d$.

The practice which has thus obtained among the merchants and traders of the Mauritius, excludes British gold and silver coins from the ordinary channels of circulation. Those channels are now, in a great measure, supplied with the rupees of the coinage of the East India Company, which, at present, constitute the principal metallic currency of the colony.

British silver coins commonly bear a premium of 4 to 6 per cent., as against the Mauritius dollar, which is reckoned equal to 2 rupees, and are used only for the purpose of paying dues and duties to the Colonial Government, and in the purchase of Commissariat Bills on the Lords of the Treasury.

A rupee contains 165 grains of fine silver, which at 5*s*. per ounce of standard silver, is worth 1*s*. 10$\frac{3}{10}$*d*.

In small dealings, the purchasing power of a British shilling is not greater than that of a half-rupee. The individual who purchases his rice, vegetables, and other necessaries, with British silver coins, suffers a loss, therefore, in his purchases, of nearly 8 per cent.

British silver, in this way, falls, in small sums, into the hands of shopkeepers, who accumulate it until it amounts to a sufficient sum—say 25*l*. or 50*l*., and then sell it to a money-broker, who disposes of it, in larger sums, and at a further profit, to the merchants, who require it for the purchase of Commissariat Bills, or for payments to the public Treasury.

CURRENCY OF CEYLON.

Previous to the year 1825, the public accounts of this island were kept in rix dollars. The currency consisted of silver rix dollars, coined at the British Mint, for the use of the colony, of copper fanams, and pice, and of incontrovertible paper rix dollars issued by the Colonial Government.

The salaries and allowances of the military and civil servants of the colony, were paid in this currency, at the rate of 1s. 6d. sterling per rix dollar. Bills drawn by the Colonial Government on the Lords of the Treasury were, at that time, generally sold by auction, at an exchange of about 15 rix dollars for 1l. sterling, showing a depreciation of the currency, compared with its professed standard, of about 10½ per cent.

In the year 1825, it was ordered that the public accounts should be kept in pounds, shillings, and pence ; the paper rix dollars were called in, and a new paper currency, expressed in the terms of sterling money, was issued by the Ceylon Treasury. The silver rix dollars, and the old coins were permitted to remain current at the rate of 1s. 6d. per rix dollar : and in the expectation of receiving a sufficient supply of British silver and copper coins from England, the Governor ordered, by proclamation, that certain foreign silver coins shall pass current, at rates fixed according to the quantity of fine silver which they were supposed respectively to contain. In this proclamation, the Spanish dollar was rated at 4s. 2d., the sicca rupee at 2s., and the Madras and Bombay rupee at 1s. 10d.

The bills drawn by the Ceylon Government on the Lords of the Treasury were afterwards sold at a fixed rate of exchange, namely, 103l. Ceylon currency for 100l. sterling; and as, at that time, the course of exchange with England, both in India and Ceylon, was in a depressed state, and in favour of England, very great facility was experienced in the negotiation of the bills.

In 1836, the currency of the island consisted mainly of British silver, and of Government paper money, convertible, at the pleasure of the holder, or with the consent of the Government, into bills on the Lords of the Treasury, at a premium of $1\frac{1}{2}$ per cent. The sicca rupee of the East India Company was, at the same time, current at the rate of 2s., being, very nearly, its value compared with silver of the British standard, at 5s. per ounce.

The current rate of exchange at Bengal upon London, was, at that period, 1s. 11d. sterling for a sicca rupee for bills at six months' sight.

In this state of the exchange, the transmission of specie was a more advantageous mode of remittance from India to Europe, than bills of exchange.

The natural tendency of the course of exchange upon London, at Ceylon, is to follow that of Bengal; but, at that period, this tendency was counteracted, by the practice of the Government of Ceylon, to redeem its outstanding notes, by bills on the Lords of the Treasury, at a premium of $1\frac{1}{2}$ per cent.

In consequence of this practice, individuals were enabled, by importing rupees from India and exchanging them at Ceylon, at the rate of 2s. each, for Government paper, or for British silver, to purchase, with Indian money, bills upon London, at a more advantageous rate of exchange at Ceylon than at Calcutta.

Thus, although the state of the exchange between India and England, induced the exportation of silver rupees from India to London, yet, at Ceylon, there was no such exportation; on the contrary, from the causes above mentioned, there was an influx into the island of Indian coins, while British silver was accumulating in the Ceylon Treasury, or was exported to other British colonies, and to England.

Under these circumstances, no difficulty was experienced in the negotiation of Government bills on the Lords of the Treasury, at a premium of $1\frac{1}{2}$ per cent.

Not long afterwards, the exchange at Calcutta, upon London, rose considerably, and continued to

rise until it was 8 or 10 per cent. above the metallic
level, in favour of India. The tide of metallic
money at Ceylon was now reversed. British silver
coins had entirely disappeared from circulation;
and it was deemed necessary by the Government
to import from India a large amount of rupees,
at a disadvantageous rate of exchange with England.

Notwithstanding this importation, the public
treasury was soon nearly exhausted of silver,
and its scarcity was inconveniently felt by the
public.

It seems to have been imagined by the Governor
and his council, that the metallic money thus in-
introduced into the colony, not by the natural
operations of commerce, but by the direct interference of the Colonial Government, would have
remained in the island, and that its retention would
have been not only convenient to the Government
but likewise productive of beneficial consequences
to the domestic industry and to the foreign trade
of the colony.

This expectation was not realized. It might,
indeed, have been foreseen, that as the rupees thus
forcibly introduced into the island were immediately used for the purpose of defraying the expenditure of the Colonial Government, they would
naturally flow back to the channels from which
they were brought, leaving no greater quantity of
money (including the Government paper) in the

island than was sufficient for the purposes of its domestic traffic.

It was, however, supposed that the difficulty of retaining in the island the money imported by the Government arose from the under-valuation of the rupee, with reference to what was supposed to be the value of the Government paper. Hence it was determined, in September, 1836, after the introduction into the colony of the new rupee of the East India Company, to give to that rupee the same nominal value as had previously been given to the sicca rupee, namely, 2s., although the new rupee is worse by $6\frac{2}{3}$ per cent. than the sicca rupee.

This measure had no other effect than that of depreciating the value of the metallic currency of the island. It enabled debtors, under existing contracts, to defraud their creditors, but did not prevent the exportation of coin. In a despatch from Governor Mackenzie, dated the 13th August, 1838, he observes, that "it is no easy matter to retain " our silver currency," and mentions that " a sum " of 10,000l. was demanded yesterday," thus showing that the retention of the East India rupees in the island was not less difficult than it had been previously to the alteration in their nominal value.

The currency of this island consists, at present, of Government paper, convertible, at the pleasure of the holder, into the coins which are legally current. The coins in circulation are principally the rupees of the East India Company, together with some British silver and copper coins, and some old silver rix dollars, current at 1*s*. 6*d*. each.

The *nominal* par of exchange with London is 1000 rupees, or 100*l*. currency for 100*l*. sterling ; but the *real* par (assuming the price of standard silver in London to be 5*s*. per ounce) is 1,076 rupees, or 107*l*. 12*s*. currency for 100*l*. sterling.

CURRENCY OF HONG KONG.

Before stating the measures which have been adopted for the regulation of the currency of this colony, it may be useful to describe the monetary system of China.

The only coin in general circulation, in China, is the *le* or *cash*, a small piece of metal composed of copper and tutenague. At each provincial city a mint is established, over which a Director is appointed by the Government. From the Board of Revenue, at Peking, coinage models are obtained. When the mint is to be worked, the Director weighs out the proper quantity of copper, and delivers it to the workmen to be cast into money, of which an amount is required to be produced by the workmen, corresponding with the quantity of copper delivered to them. It frequently happens, however, that the workmen throw sand into the model, together with the metal, and are thus enabled to purloin the copper.

The weight of each piece of the money should be one mace; its value, as fixed by Government, is one thousandth part of a tael's weight of silver; but in consequence of adulteration and illicit coinage, 1200 to 1400 cash are commonly given for a tael.

The native silver of China, called Sycee, passes

in exchange by weight, and is always required by the Government in the receipt of taxes.

When the officers of the several departments are desirous of paying over to the heads of the Government, the revenue arising from the land-tax and the duties on merchandize, they apply to a banker, and obtain the required amount in fine silver, compensating the banker for whatever difference there may be between its value and that of the money which they bring to his shop.

Those bankers are furnished with furnaces, in which the metal is fused ; after melting, it is poured into clay moulds, and formed into ingots of various forms and weights, most commonly of ten taels each. Upon the ingot is marked the year, and the district in which it was issued, together with the names of the workmen, and of the shop where it was cast. Should any deception be afterwards discovered, at whatever distance of time, the refiner is subject to severe punishment.*

Sycee silver is divided into several classes, according to its fineness ; the kinds most current in the province of Canton are the following :—

1. Kwan-reang, the hoppo's duties, or the silver which is forwarded to the Imperial Treasury at Peking. This is always of 97 to 99 touch. On all the Imperial duties, a certain per centage is levied, for the purpose of turning them into Sycee

* Bridgman's Chinese Chrestomathy.

of this high standard, and the expense of conveying the silver to Peking.

2. Fan-koo or fan-foo, the treasurer's receipts, or the silver in which the land-tax is paid. This is also of high standard, but inferior to that of the hoppo's duties; and being intended for use in the province, no per centage is levied for the expense of conveyance.

3. Yuen-poou or une-po, literally, chief in value. This kind is usually imported from Soodron, in large pieces of fifty taels each.

4. Yen, or cem, heang, salt duties. This class is inferior only to

5. Wech, or mut-tae, the name of which signifies " uncleansed" or "unpurified."*

The Sycee silver paid by the Chinese Government to the British authorities at Canton, under the treaty of Nanking, and imported into Her Majesty's Mint, was found, on assay, to be rather more than 13 dwts. better than silver of the British standard, (or 97·05 touch) and to contain on an average, $13\frac{1}{3}$ grains of fine gold in each pound, troy weight, of silver.

Sycee silver of the same description (being likewise part of the Chinese indemnity) imported into the East Company's Mint at Bombay, was found to be of rather superior fineness to that imported into Her Majesty's Mint in London, being very nearly 98 touch.

* Morrison's Chinese Commercial Guide.

The following is a comparative statement of the produce of 1000 taels of Sycee silver imported into the Mints of London and Bombay.

LONDON MINT.

The produce of 1000 taels delivered at the Royal Mint was 1207·57 ounces, which were found, on assay, to be equal to 1276·23 ounces of silver, of the British standard, of which

The Sale produce was	£320	12	0
The value of the fine gold contained in 1000 taels of Sycee (over and above 5 grains per lb. allowed to the buyer of the silver) was	7	9	9
Sale produce of 1000 taels of Sycee silver	£328	1	9

BOMBAY MINT.

The produce of 1000 taels delivered at the Bombay Mint was $1293\frac{7}{10}$ ounces troy weight of silver of the Indian Mint standard, equal to $3449\frac{8}{10}$ Tola weight, or—

	Rupees.	An.	Pice.
Company's rupees	3,449	12	10
Deduct Indian Mint charge of 2 per cent.	70	4	10
Coinage produce of 1000 taels of Sycee silver	3,379	8	0

In order to ascertain the net proceeds, it would be necessary to deduct from the above stated results, freight, insurance, shipping, and landing charges ; but as these were nearly the same in both cases, it may be concluded that the same quantity of Sycee silver, which produced 1s. $11\frac{3}{10}d.$, ster-

ling in London, produced one rupee of the coinage
of the East India Company at Bombay.

The nominal monies of China are the leang,
tseen, and fun, commonly called by foreigners, tael,
mace, and candareen, the proportion of which to
each other is decimal. The candareen, in accounts,
is reckoned equal to 10 le or cash ; but, as is above
stated, owing to adulteration and illicit coinage,
12 or 14 cash are commonly given for a candareen.

The terms tael, mace, and candareen, are denominations of *weight,* but are commonly used as
denominations of *money.* The weight of 100 taels
is equal to 120 ounces, 16 cwts. of English troy
weight, or 579·84 grains per tael.

The circulating medium of Canton consists of
chopped or broken Spanish dollars, the number of
which that go to a tael differs in different trades,
and amongst different classes of persons, according
to long-established usages.

In *calculations* and *accounts,* taels are converted
into dollars, at the rate of 720 per 1000 dollars.

But payments in *cash* are generally *weighed* at
717 per 1000 dollars.

Payments for Bengal opium, at 718 per 1000 dollars. Native merchants, not of the cohong, unless
it be otherwise specially agreed, receive payments
at 715 per 1000 dollars.

Payments into the Treasury of the East India Company were made at 718 per 1000 dollars.

Payments at Macao are usually at 720 per 1000 dollars.*

When payment of 1000 dollars is required to be made, the payment is effected in this way : in one scale is placed the weight of 717 taels (for example), and in the other, as many dollars as are sufficient to counterbalance that weight.

Hence it may happen that more or less than 1000 dollars, by tale, are required to discharge an obligation to pay 1000 dollars.

Dollars, though of the same weight and purity, are not received alike by the Chinese ; the difference chiefly arises from caprice, so that what is preferred in one place is often refused at another place, unless at a discount.

Spanish dollars known by the name of pillar dollars, if uninjured by the Canton practice of stamping, bear a premium varying from 1 to $1\frac{1}{2}$ per cent. There are other dollars bearing the stamp of the letter G, to denote their being coined at the Guadaljara Mint, which are never received but at a discount. South American and United States dollars do not pass among the Chinese.†

The Spanish dollar of the coinage of Ferdinand is, at present, regarded at Canton as the standard to which all money contracts have reference.

* Morrison's Chinese Commercial Guide.
† *Ibid.*

Compared with this coin, the dollars of Mexico and South America are commonly at a discount, varying from 3 to 7 per cent.; Sycee silver at a premium of 1 to 5 per cent., and the dollars of the coinage of Carolus IV., at a premium varying from 4 to 12 per cent.

On the 29th March, 1842, a proclamation was issued by Sir Henry Pottinger, at Hong Kong, ordering that in the common bazaar, purchases, barter, hire, &c. in that Island, dollars of whatsoever denomination, whether whole or chopped, shall circulate at par with reference to each other, provided that they are of the proper weight and standard.

It was further ordered that $2\frac{1}{4}$ rupees of the East India Company shall be considered equal to one dollar; that 1200 copper cash shall likewise be considered equal to one dollar, and that 533 cash shall be considered equal to one rupee.

In this proclamation the dollar, and the East India Company's rupee, may be considered as correctly rated relatively to each other, when regard is had only to the pure silver which those coins respectively contain; but as, in consequence of the Indian Mint charge of 2 per cent. for coinage, $2\frac{1}{4}$ rupees are worth more in India than one dollar; and as rupees, so rated, afford a more advantageous medium of remittance from Hong Kong to India than dollars, the former coins, whenever that object is in contemplation, will naturally be preferred to the latter.

On the 27th April, 1842, another proclamation was published at Hong Kong, directing that Mexican and other Republican dollars shall be taken, and considered to be the standard in all Government and mercantile transactions at Hong Kong, and other places in China in the occupation of Her Majesty's forces, unless at the time of such transactions taking place it should be expressly agreed to the contrary.

This extension of Mexican and other Republican dollars to Government and mercantile, as well as to bazaar, transactions, it was expected would lead to an abolition of the distinction which prevails amongst the Chinese between different kinds of dollars, and of their preference of one kind to another. It does not, however, appear to have produced that effect. Mexican and South American dollars are still regarded as inferior to those of the coinage of Ferdinand, and still more so to those of the coinage of Carolus IV.*

After the erection of Hong Kong into a British colony, it was determined to extend to that island the same regulations, with regard to its currency, as were in force in all the British colonies and

---

* The Chinese are very fastidious in the choice of coins, rejecting some and choosing others, merely with regard to the device. Spanish dollars, with pillars, especially those issued in the reign of Charles IV., are the most current, often bearing a slight premium ; while on the other hand, the coins of all the American States are passed with difficulty, at a discount of 2, 3, and even 6 per cent.—*Bridgman's Chinese Chrestomathy.*

possessions, except the territories of the East India Company and Ceylon.

An Order in Council and a proclamation were accordingly prepared, in order to give effect to that determination; which order and proclamation were afterwards published in due course by the governor of the colony, and are now in force.

This proclamation, after reciting the proclamations issued by Sir Henry Pottinger on the 27th March, and the 27th April, 1842, declares and ordains the revocation and annulment of those proclamations; and further ordains that from and after its publication the several coins therein specified, being perfect coins, and of full and proper weight and value, shall, in like manner as the gold, silver, and copper coins of the United Kingdom, be a legal tender at the under-mentioned rates; that is to say,—

The gold mohur of the East India Company's territory, coined since the 1st day of September, 1835, at the rate of twenty-nine shillings and two-pence sterling money of the United Kingdom.

The dollar of Spain, Mexico, or the South American States, at the rate of four shillings and two pence sterling.

The rupee of the East India Company's territory, coined since the 1st day of September, 1835, at the rate of one shilling and ten pence sterling; and the half rupee, quarter rupee, and eighth of rupee pieces, in proportion.

The cash, or copper coin current in China, at the rate of two hundred and eighty-eight cash for one shilling sterling.

The proclamation further ordains that tenders of payment in the said coins, as well as in the gold, silver, or copper coins of the United Kingdom, according to the several relative rates and values above specified, shall be deemed and taken, within the island of Hong Kong and its dependencies, to be a sufficient and lawful tender in satisfaction of all debts, contracts, and engagements whatsoever for the payment of money : provided that it shall not be compulsory on any person to accept, at any one payment, a larger amount in silver coins of the United Kingdom of lower denomination than one shilling, or in the half, quarter, or eighth rupee pieces than the equivalent to twenty shillings sterling money, or a larger amount in copper coins of the United Kingdom, or in Chinese copper coins, than the equivalent to one shilling sterling money.

Under the regulations established by this proclamation, all pecuniary contracts and engagements entered into at Hong Kong and its dependencies in the terms of the sterling money of the United Kingdom, may be legally discharged with any of the coins specified in it at the rates respectively assigned to them.

Agreements at Hong Kong to pay a certain amount of "dollars," may now be discharged by the payment of gold sovereigns at the rate of 4 dollars and 80 cents, or of rupees at the rate of 44 cents, or of British shillings at the rate of 24 cents.

The rules laid down in Her Majesty's proclamation, will, it may be expected, facilitate transactions amongst the inhabitants of Hong Kong and its dependencies, without occasioning any difficulty or embarrassment in money transactions with the Chinese at Canton and other places in China. At Hong Kong the dollars of Ferdinand will be said to be at a premium, as compared with those of Mexico. At Canton, Mexican dollars will be quoted at a discount as compared with those of the coinage of Ferdinand; but it is not likely that this difference of expression will lead to any practical inconvenience or misunderstanding.

The object constantly kept in view in the alterations that have been made, and the regulations which have been established with respect to the currency of the colonies, since the year 1798, was to prepare the way, and to facilitate the establishment in them of the coins and money denominations of the mother country without disturbing existing contracts, and with as little interference as possible with the prejudices and habits of the people.

This has been finally accomplished at Jamaica, Bermuda, the Australian colonies, and Van Diemen's Land. The rates of the foreign coins in circulation having first been correctly rated relatively to each other in the current denominations of those colonies, the transition to the sterling denominations of the United Kingdom was effected without difficulty.

A similar change may now be made with the same facility, in all the colonial possessions of the Crown, and it may reasonably be expected that the advantage of such a change will be perceived by the colonists, and the measures necessary for its attainment be adopted.

APPENDIX.

Copy of Treasury Minute, dated 11*th February,*
1825.

My Lords have under their consideration the State
of the Currencies in the several British Colonies and
Possessions abroad, as they affect the Expenditure for the
public service, both military and civil.

They consider it as being highly expedient that they
should avail themselves of the present period of peace,
and of the means which appear to be now at their disposal, for introducing a fixed and uniform medium of
exchange for all transactions connected with the public
service, in the place of the various, fluctuating, and
anomalous currencies which have been created under the
pressure of temporary emergency, or with views of local
and peculiar expediency, in many of these colonies and
possessions during the war; and which have been productive of much private and public inconvenience.

In these colonies the Spanish dollar has generally been
the prevalent current coin, and the standard by which
the value of other currencies, whether metallic or paper,
has been determined.

That coin has been the medium of payment to the
troops on Foreign stations generally; but the rate in
sterling money at which it has been issued to the Army,
has not been the same at all of those stations, nor has that

rate in any case been fixed in conformity with the intrinsic value of the coin.

In the West Indies, in America, on the western coast of Africa, at the Cape of Good Hope, at the Mauritius, and at New South Wales, it has been reckoned in payment to the Army at 4s. 8d.; while at Gibraltar and in the Mediterranean, it has been issued at 4s. 6d.

At some of these places, payments are made to the forces in other coins than Spanish dollars; but in those cases the value of such coins has been regulated by the Spanish dollar, assuming the value of the latter at the army-rate fixed for each station.

These established rates are of long standing, and many of them founded upon authorities, of the origin of which there are no distinct records in this office.

The intrinsic value of the Spanish dollar as compared with British standard silver, at the mint price of 5s. 2d. the ounce, is about 4s. 3.79d. or somewhat less than 4s. 4d.; and at the market prices of silver which have prevailed for some time past, it is scarcely above 4s.

It appears, therefore, that the prices at which dollars are now issued to the British troops abroad, are considerably higher than the real value of the coin, or its value in British money at the mint price of silver; and the Army would have cause to complain if they had not antecedently, during a great length of time, enjoyed the advantage of receiving that coin at a rate much below the value into which it was convertible in British currency through the medium of the exchanges.

Remonstrances have, however, proceeded from several of the Foreign stations, on behalf of the Army, on account of the rates at which the dollar is now issued; and although the change by which a more correct issue of the pay of the troops abroad must be introduced, will unavoidably be attended with a considerable increase of expense, My Lords deem it just and necessary to adopt measures for that purpose.

They must at the same time observe, that by the regulations adopted for the pay of the regimental officers, that valuable class of the public servants, who would otherwise be the most seriously affected by the disadvantages of this army-rate of exchange, are wholly freed from its inconveniences, as they have for many years past enjoyed the option of receiving their pay either from the military chest, at the station where they are serving, or through their agents in England ; by which means they have the full benefit of the state of the exchange when it is more favourable than the army-rate, and the advantage of the army-rate when it is less so. The inconvenience has, therefore, since that regulation, been confined to the officers on the staff, and some others who, as well as the private men, receive their pay from the military chest alone, and who are in some degree indemnified by the mode in which those supplies in kind are procured for them, which to a certain extent are defrayed by stoppages from their pay.

In considering this subject, with a view to the introduction of a better mode of paying the Army abroad, My Lords advert to the circumstances which affect the supply of the Spanish dollar at the present time. Some difficulties in procuring it in sufficient quantities, are occasioned by the diminished produce of the mines; while, on the other hand, the established character of that coin, on account of its formerly well-known uniformity of weight and fineness, has been materially affected by diversities lately introduced in the coinage in America : whereby it has been rendered less fit for the payments which are now under consideration.

Under these circumstances, it appears to My Lords that the fittest medium for the payment of the forces, and the best standard of circulation for the British colonies and possessions where these anomalies have hitherto prevailed, will be the silver and copper currencies now in circulation in this country, provided the same be made convertible, at the will of the holder, into the standard gold currency of the United Kingdom, by means of bills of exchange, to be given at a rate to be fixed for each station by the officer in charge of the military chest, or some other public authority.

Owing to the rate at which silver is by the Act 56 Geo. III, c. 68, converted into coin at the mint (which is considerably above its general market value, as well as its former mint price,) this currency would not be liable to be withdrawn by private speculation, from the colonies; while, on the other hand, its ready convertibility, by the means above mentioned, into that money which is the legal tender for large payments in this country, would secure its circulation at the same value in the colonies.

As there would exist no inducement to export a currency of this description to foreign countries, so, on the other hand, if the rate at which bills would be obtainable for it upon England, be fixed in such manner as to be about equal to the expense and risk of bringing it to England, the danger of any inconvenience from its re-importation into this country, would in like manner be avoided.

This rate My Lords conceive to be about 3 per cent. from almost all of the stations to which these measures would be applicable; and they would therefore direct, in the first instance generally, that the officer in charge of the commissariat should give a bill for £100 on this Board for every £103 in British silver currency; such rate being subject to future regulation in any case in which it may, on experience, be found to be too high, or too low, for the purpose which it is intended to secure.

Upon these grounds, therefore, My Lords will direct supplies of silver coin to be prepared for remittance to the several stations abroad, so as to furnish a sufficiency for the probable wants of each as speedily as possible. They desire that the agent for commissariat supplies will take the necessary steps for that purpose.

But as the substitution of this currency for the Spanish dollar, even in the payments from the military chest to the troops, can only be gradually effected, and as it may, in many cases, be still expedient to employ that coin as a medium of payment, at a fixed rate as compared with British currency, My Lords are of opinion that it should (when necessary) be issued at the rate of 4s. 4d. the dollar, being a fraction of a farthing only above its intrinsic value at the rate of 5s. 2d. the ounce of standard silver; and also, that all other coins in use in the colonies should, if used under any special expediency for making payments from the military chest, be issued at the same rate, as nearly as may be, with reference to their intrinsic value as compared with that of the Spanish dollar.

Their Lordships desire that letters be written to the commanders of the forces, and to the officers in charge of the commissariat, on each station abroad, conveying to them the necessary instructions for carrying this measure into execution, and directing that the rate at which the Spanish dollar and other coins are hereafter to be issued for the pay of the Troops, be adopted from the 24th of the month next succeeding the receipt of the instructions.

Let the attention of the commanders of the forces be called to the rates at which certain allowances in money are made within their respective commands for forage, lodging, &c. &c. which, having been fixed in British money with reference both to the expense of the articles, and to the value of the currency in which the payments were made, will require a revision upon the introduction of the changes hereby directed. They desire, therefore, that Boards may be appointed at each station for inquiring into the subject of these allowances, and for reporting what alterations should be made in their nominal sterling rates, so as to keep the real amount of them at least as low as they are at present, for which purpose the reduction must in all cases be equal to the difference between the present army-rate of the dollar and the proposed new rate of 4s. 4d. for that coin.

Let the officer in charge of the commissariat be also instructed, that all unliquidated engagements with contractors or other persons, are to be completed according to the terms of those engagements; but that in all future contracts the commissariat should reserve to itself the option of paying the contractor either in British silver or in bills upon this Board, at the rate above stated of £100 in such bills for every £103 in money: And, further, My Lords desire that the commissaries be directed not to grant bills on any occasion for British money at any other rate.

If at any time there should not be a sufficiency of British silver at the disposal of any commissary, for carrying on the service at his station, he is then to advertise for Spanish dollars or other coins, by public competition, for his bills on this Board, and is to accept the lowest tender; the dollars or coins so purchased to be issued invariably to the Troops at the rate of 4s. 4d. for the Spanish dollar, and at proportionate rates for other coins, according to their intrinsic values as compared with the Spanish dollar valued at that rate.

Let copies of this Minute be transmitted to the Commander-in-Chief of the forces, and to the Comptrollers of Army Accounts, for their information; and also to the Master-General and Board of Ordnance, and to the

Lords of the Admiralty; in order that the former may give instructions for the issue of pay to the officers and men of the several establishments under their orders abroad, in conformity with these regulations; and that the latter may give similar directions, through the paymaster of the Marines, with respect to the detachment stationed at Bermuda; to whom it appears that their pay is now issued in dollars at the rate of $4/5\frac{1}{3}$ sterling per dollar. My Lords presume that the Board of Admiralty will think it right to put that detachment upon the same footing hereafter as the Troops of the line, with respect to the issue of their pay, and the stoppages to be made from it.

Transmit copy of this Minute also to Mr. Wilmot Horton, for the information of Lord Bathurst; and request he will move his Lordship to cause the necessary communications of the measures hereby directed to be made to the governors of the several colonies, together with such instructions as may appear to his Lordship to be proper for ensuring a due attention on the part of those governors to the execution of them. Desire also, that he will move Lord Bathurst to point out to the governors of Nova Scotia and Demerara the expediency of taking some measures for the gradual reduction of the paper circulation, issued for colonial purposes and under colonial authority in those colonies, and of making it exchangeable, until it be finally reduced to that which it purports to represent.

With respect to the currencies which now constitute the chief circulating medium at New South Wales, Sierra Leone, the Mauritius, Ceylon, and the Cape of Good Hope, some more special directions appear to be necessary, in order to the introduction of the measures which are the subject of this Minute into those colonies.

NEW SOUTH WALES.

The Accounts are kept in the British denomination of money, namely, pounds, shillings, and pence, but there are few, if any, British coins circulating. The Spanish dollar being the next ordinary and common medium of exchange, and which passes at various values with reference to the pound sterling, according to the transaction to which it is applied. The Spanish dollar in private transactions of trade and commerce is rated at . . . . 5s.

In payment to the troops . . . 4s. 8d.
In payment of salaries to civil servants 4s.
In payment by the government for supplies 5s.
In payment to the government, for duties, at the average rate of exchange.

This state of things appears to My Lords to be highly objectionable; and they are of opinion that it would be expedient to provide that all debts which may be contracted, and all engagements which may be made, after a day to be named for the payment of money in the colony, should be discharged either in British silver money, or in Spanish dollars at 4s. 4d. each, at the will of the debtor; and that the Spanish dollar should also be issued and paid, in all government transactions, at the same rate.

That all engagements contracted previously to the day to be so named, either by the government or by individuals, shall be respectively discharged and liquidated by the payment of 17s. 4d. in the pound for the nominal amount of the debt, either in British silver money, or in dollars computed at 4s. 4d. each; by which a debt already contracted will be discharged by the same number of dollars as at present.* If at any time it should be absolutely necessary to introduce into circulation any other description of coin than British or Spanish dollars and their proportions, the value at which it should be taken should be accurately fixed with reference to the quantity of fine silver contained therein, as compared to the quantity contained in British standard silver at 5s. 2d. per oz., or in Spanish dollars at 4s. 4d. each :—a Statement of which, with respect to several of the coins, My Lords have caused to be extracted from the tables of assay recently made at the mints, both of London and Paris, and which have been found to verify each other.

SIERRA LEONE.

The Accounts are kept, as at New South Wales, in the British denominations of money, and the dollar is in all transactions of commerce taken at 5s. each, and is issued to the troops at 4s. 8d. My Lords are therefore of opinion, that it would be expedient to provide that all debts which may be contracted, and all engagements which may be made, after a day to be named for the payment of money, should be discharged either in British silver money, or in Spanish dollars at 4s. 4d. each, at the will of the debtor ; and the latter coin should after that day be issued and received in all government payments on account of government, at the same rate of 4s. 4d. each. But it should be provided, that all engagements already contracted, either by the government or by individuals, should be respectively discharged and liquidated by the payment of 17s. 4d. in the pound for the nominal amount of the debt, either in British silver

---

* Debt of 100l. discharged by 400 dollars at 5s. each. Debt of 100l. to be paid at 17s. 4d. in the pound, would amount to 86l. 13s. 4d. and which debt would require 400 dollars for its discharge, computed at 4s. 4d. each.

money, or dollars computed at 4s. 4d. each, by which the debt already contracted will be discharged by the same number of dollars as at present.

MAURITIUS.

The Currency has chiefly been Spanish dollars, and paper dollars supposed to be of the same value as Spanish dollars; but these paper dollars have been at various times considerably depreciated. Instructions however have recently been transmitted to the Mauritius, which provide, if not for the immediate liquidation of the whole of the paper dollars, at least for raising their value to that of the Spanish dollar, and for their gradual reduction. It may therefore be stated, that the general circulation is Spanish dollars and various coins of India; and when the dollar is quoted with reference to British money, it is called equal to 5s. The various coins of India are valued in circulation with reference to the Spanish dollar at that rate.

The Spanish dollars (and other coins in proportion) are issued to the troops at 4s. 8d., and to the civil servants at the same rate.

My Lords are of opinion that currency should be given to the British silver coin, and that any debt in dollars should be considered as discharged by a payment in Spanish dollars, or in British money at the rate of 4s. 4d. British money for each dollar; and that in all cases where it may be necessary to issue Spanish dollars to civil or military servants, for salaries, or otherwise, they should be issued at the rate of 4s. 4d. each; and that all other silver coins usually circulating at the Mauritius, should be issued at a fixed value, with reference to their intrinsic value as compared with British standard silver, at 5s. 2d. per oz, troy, or with Spanish dollars at 4s. 4d. each. It further appears to My Lords, that it would be expedient to form tariffs of the duties now payable to the Crown in British money, and to impose all new duties in the same currency, leaving the parties to pay the same in any other coin authorized to circulate in the Mauritius at the established rates by which the accounts of the government may be immediately kept in the denomination of British money. A provision should also be made, similar to that proposed with respect to New South Wales and Sierra Leone, for payment of any debts which may have been contracted previously to a day to be named, in money of British denomination; but which debts are by usage payable in dollars at 5s. each.

CAPE OF GOOD HOPE.

The Spanish dollar was formerly issued to the Troops at this station universally, and at the rate of 4s. 8d. each, but they never obtained any considerable general circulation ; and latterly their use has been almost discontinued in issues to the Troops, who have been paid in the paper rix dollar computed at the current rate of exchange. There is, in fact, at present no metallic circulation at this colony, and the paper money is not exchangeable against any metallic money, nor has it any real fixed value with reference to metallic money. The nominal value of the rix dollar is 4s. but it has for many years been at a very considerable discount in exchange for bills upon England, and its real value, with reference to those bills, has not, upon an average of two or three years, been more than 1s. 6d. sterling. My Lords feel that it would be inexpedient, if not impossible, to introduce a metallic currency into this colony, without either providing for the immediate payment of the whole of this paper money, or fixing a rate at which it should be received both in public and private transactions, and made exchangeable by the

Government, at the will of the holder, for metallic money, or for bills upon this Board. With reference to the average rate of exchange, as above stated, it appears to My Lords, that 1s. 6d. per rix dollar may be considered as a fair rate, and they are therefore of opinion the rix dollar should be declared equal to 1s. 6d. in British silver money; and with a view to prevent it from falling below that rate, that it shall be at all times exchangeable, at the will of the holder, for bills upon this Board, at the rate of 103l. in value of rix dollars computed at 1s. 6d. each for every 100l. bill; and that after the arrival of a sufficient amount of British metallic money in the colony, no paper brought in to be exchanged for bills upon this Board should be re-issued, but that such paper money should be cancelled, and wholly withdrawn from circulation, and that none other in lieu thereof should thereafter be issued. And it is their Lordships' opinion, that the paper money withdrawn from circulation should be sent to this country, as vouchers for the bills which may be drawn on account of it. By this measure, it is presumed that the value of the paper money will be maintained at its fixed rate, with reference to British money.

The number of paper rix dollars in circulation, which have been from time to time issued at the Cape of Good Hope, is about 3,108,000; and the total amount of bills upon this Board, if the whole were to be exchanged for such bills, would therefore be about the sum of 226,000l. But as a part of those rix dollars were issued by a government establishment, called the Lombard Bank, upon various securities, the sums which may from time to time be paid upon these securities, should be applied towards the liquidation of this paper money. It is not, however, their Lordships' intention that any compulsory measures should be taken to withdraw the whole of the paper money from circulation; but that such portions only should be cancelled as may from time to time be brought in by individuals in exchange for bills upon this Board ; and that the paper money which may be received for rates, taxes, or other revenues, should be again issued in payment of the current expenditure, except such paper money as may represent a less sum than 10 rix dollars, which should not, after the arrival of British metallic money, be re-issued, but should be cancelled, and sent home as vouchers to the accounts, as should also rix dollars equal in amount to the sum paid to the Lombard Bank, in liquidation of the debts due to that establishment.

As the rates, taxes, &c., are at present imposed in this colony in rix dollars, and as it appears to My Lords that it would be extremely convenient to introduce into all the colonies belonging to the United Kingdom the same description of money, My Lords are of opinion, that it would be expedient to establish a new Schedule of rates, duties, &c., payable to the Crown, in which Schedule the present rates in rix dollars, and the new rates in British money, at the proposed fixed rate of the rix dollar, should be specified ; and that all collectors and other officers of government at the Cape of Good Hope should be required to render their accounts in British money.

CEYLON.

The Currency of this Island is very various, and consists of rix dollars coined in England for its use, of many of the coins of India, of Spanish dollars, and of paper rix dollars.

The rix dollar coined in England expressly for the use of Ceylon, is rated very much above its intrinsic worth, measured by British currency ; and neither that or the paper rix dollar is exchangeable at the will of the holder, at its nominal rate against British money, or any other description of coin. The consequence naturally is, that in all transactions of exchange, the silver rix dollar is rated with reference to its intrinsic and not to its nominal value, and a very considerable depreciation of this coin appears to exist. Of this depreciation, numerous complaints have been made from the civil and military servants of the colony, who receive their salaries in this description of currency at its nominal rate; but, as some compensation for the loss which they sustain, they are permitted to exchange a certain portion of their salary, or rather to receive it, in debentures or in bills payable in Great Britain, which are granted at the nominal par. The rix dollars last coined in Great Britain were equal in weight and fineness to one-third of a Spanish dollar; consequently, taking the Spanish dollar at 4s. 4d., they are worth only 1s. 5¾d., although they are nominally rated at 1s. 9d. It appears to My Lords, that the value of the rix dollar should be rated more nearly to its intrinsic worth as compared to the Spanish dollar, and that the silver rix dollar, as well as the paper rix dollar, should be made exchangeable at the will of the holder, at such reduced value, either for British coins or for bills upon this Board. My Lords are therefore of opinion, that the value of the silver and paper rix dollar should be fixed at 1s. 6d.; and in order to prevent the paper rix dollar from falling below that value, that an authority should be conveyed to the governor, to draw bills upon the agent of the island in England, in sums of not less than 100l. for any amount of paper rix dollars which may be tendered at the colonial treasury, at the rate of 103l. value of rix dollars for every 100l. bill; and that instructions should be sent to the governor, that the paper rix dollar so brought in for bills should be cancelled, and transmitted to this country as vouchers for the bills drawn; and that none other in lieu thereof should be issued to replace the paper money thus withdrawn from circulation, by which measure, it is to be presumed that the value of this paper money, while any part of it remains in circulation, will be maintained at its fixed rates with reference to British money, and will be gradually paid off and cancelled.

The number of paper rix dollars in circulation and issued upon the credit of the government, and the amount of debentures bearing various rates of interest, which have been issued in exchange for those rix dollars, is about 4,041,900 ; and the total amount of the bills to be drawn, if the whole were to be exchanged for such bills, would be about the sum of 296,000*l.*; but a part of that sum will be supplied from the funds appropriated as sinking fund for the redemption of those rix dollars, and even the remainder will be gradually drawn for, as it is not their Lordships' intention that any compulsory measures should be taken to withdraw the whole of the paper money from circulation; and that the paper money which may be received by government for rates, taxes, &c., should be again issued in payment of the current expenditure.

It appears to My Lords, that after the promulgation of these orders, neither the civil nor military servants of the colony should receive bills upon England upon any other terms than other individuals, namely, for Spanish dollars or other coins at the current or market rate of exchange ; and for British money, or for metal or paper rix dollars, at the rate of a bill of 100*l.* for every 103*l.* of British silver coin, or metal or paper rix dollars.

The rates, taxes, &c., in this Island being at present imposed in rix dollars, My Lords deem it expedient that the same arrangement should be adopted in respect thereof as that proposed for the Cape of Good Hope, namely, that a new Schedule of all the rates, duties, &c., payable to the Crown, should be framed ; in which Schedule the present rates in rix dollars, and new rates in British money, at the proposed fixed rate of the rix dollar, should be specified, and that all collectors and other officers of the government at Ceylon should be required to render their accounts in British money.

My Lords further think, that from the date of the receipt of their instructions, no debenture bearing interest payable in Ceylon, or in this country, should upon any account be granted; and that the governor should be instructed to transmit an account of those now outstanding, distinguishing those the interest of which is payable in Ceylon, from those the interest of which is payable in Great Britain; and specifying also the conditions upon which the debentures were issued, and the periods when they will become payable, in order that such arrangements may be made, with the aid of the sinking fund established for the liquidation of these debentures, as may ensure their liquidation at the time they may respectively become due.

Transmit copy of this Minute to Mr. Wilmot Horton, for the information and consideration of the Earl Bathurst; and request he will inform My Lords if his Lordship concurs in the proposed measures; and if so, whether, in his opinion, application should be made for an Order of His Majesty in Council, for giving effect to these arrangements in the colonies of New South Wales, Mauritius, Ceylon, Cape of Good Hope, and Sierra Leone; or whether the same may be more conveniently carried into effect by his Lordship's directions to the governors of these several colonies to issue proclamations for carrying these arrangements into effect.

(Copy.)

SIR,   Downing-street, 28th February 1825.

I HAVE laid before Earl Bathurst your letter of the 12th instant, transmitting a Minute of the Board of Treasury relative to the introduction of the British silver

currency into the Colonies belonging to the United Kingdom, under certain regulations therein detailed; and I
am to acquaint you in reply, that Lord Bathurst entirely
approves of the measures proposed by their Lordships,
and is of opinion that it would be advisable to give effect
to the arrangement by an Order of His Majesty in
Council.

I am, &c.

(Signed)   R. J. W. HORTON.

Geo. Harrison, Esq.
&c. &c. &c.

AT THE COURT AT CARLTON HOUSE,—23d March, 1825;

Present, The KING'S MOST EXCELLENT MAJESTY in
Council.

Whereas it has been represented to His Majesty at
this Board, by the Lords Commissioners of His Majesty's
Treasury, that they have given directions that His
Majesty's Troops serving in the several British colonies
and possessions abroad, should in certain cases be paid in
British silver and copper money ; and that with a view of
securing the circulation of such money in those colonies,
it would be expedient that an Order in Council should
be issued declaring, that in all those colonies where the
Spanish dollar is now, either by law, fact, or practice,
considered as a legal tender for the discharge of debts, or
where the duties to the government are rated or collected,
or the individuals have a right to pay in that description
of coin, that a tender and payment of British silver money
to the amount of four shillings and four pence, should be
considered as equivalent to the tender or payment of one
Spanish dollar, and so in proportion for any greater or
less amount of debt : And whereas it has been further
represented by the Lords Commissioners of His Majesty's

Treasury, that with respect to the Cape of Good Hope, where there are not any Spanish dollars in circulation, but where the circulation consists entirely of paper rix dollars and its proportions; and with respect to Ceylon, where the circulation consists of silver and paper rix dollars, as well as of a variety of other coins which are generally received and paid with relation to their value as compared with rix dollars, it would be expedient that a tender and payment of 1s. 6d. in British silver money should be considered as equivalent to a tender and payment of one such rix dollar so current at the Cape of Good Hope and Ceylon respectively, and so in proportion for any greater or less sum; and also that British copper should be made a legal tender in all the British colonies, for its due and proper proportions of British silver money, as by law established in Great Britain, but that no person should be compelled to take more than 12d. in copper money at any one payment :—His Majesty, having taken the said representation into consideration, is pleased, by and with the advice of His Privy Council, to approve of what is therein proposed ; and the Right Honourable the Lords Commissioners of His Majesty's Treasury, and the Right Honourable Earl Bathurst, one of His Majesty's Principal Secretaries of State, are to give the necessary directions herein, as to them may respectively appertain.

(Signed)   C. C. GREVILLE.

ROYAL ORDERS AND PROCLAMATIONS RELATING TO
COINS AND CURRENCY.

WEST INDIES.

(*Circular.*)

SIR,   Downing-street, September, 1838.

THE state of the currency in the West Indies has,
for some time past, engaged the serious attention of Her
Majesty's Government.

The very unsatisfactory state of the monetary system
in those colonies, the almost total disappearance of the
Spanish dollar from the ordinary channels of circulation,
the substitution of mutilated coins, or of parts of coins,
and the difficulty of preserving even these, defective as
they are, in sufficient quantity for the purposes of domestic interchange, warranted the apprehension that in the
constitution and structure of the colonial currency there
exists some original error, without the correction of
which that currency cannot be placed on a just foundation, or retained in a sound and satisfactory state.

From the inquiry instituted on this subject, it appears
that the main error of the system, the principal source
of the actual inconvenience, consists in the over-valuation of the gold coins in circulation relatively to those of
silver.

In the general market of the commercial world, the
proportionate value of silver to gold is very nearly 15·8
to 1.

In the West Indies, although the nominal currencies of
the different islands vary considerably from each other,
the doubloon of Mexico and South America, whatever

may be the law in particular islands, is in practice taken to be equivalent to 16 dollars; which makes the proportionate value of fine silver to fine gold, as nearly as can be computed from the average weight and fineness of those coins, as ascertained by the Assay Master of Her Majesty's Mint, very nearly 16·48 to 1.

This over-valuation of the doubloon has rendered gold the ultimate standard to which all money contracts in the West Indies have reference ; for although, according to the original meaning of the terms in which the money of account is expressed, silver is the commodity intended to be conveyed, in all pecuniary contracts, yet the words which were once understood to mean a certain quantity of silver, now mean either that quantity of silver or a certain quantity of gold ; and as a debtor always chooses to acquit himself of his obligation by a payment in the cheaper metal, or in coins of that metal which are over-rated with reference to those of the other, both parties to the contract must, at the time of entering into it, have contemplated a payment in gold.

Under the circumstances which I have stated, the dollar and the doubloon cannot be maintained in concurrent circulation at the proportionate rates of 16·48 to 1, assigned to them by law or practice.

In the general market of the world, the relative value of the two coins is understood to be in the proportion of about $15\frac{1}{2}$ to 1.

In London the value of a Mexican dollar, estimated in the gold currency of the United Kingdom, is now, and has been for some time past, very nearly 4s. 2d.

The value of a doubloon at the Mint price of 3l. 17s. $10\frac{1}{2}d$. per oz. for gold of the British standard (assuming the doubloon to contain 362 grains of fine gold) is very nearly 64s.

The proportion of 4s. 2d. to 64s. is as 1 to 15·36.

This proportion Her Majesty's Government have taken as the basis of the alteration which, with the view of rendering the concurrent circulation of the dollar and the doubloon practicable, they have deemed it proper to make.

In the application of this rule of proportion to the currencies of the different islands of the West Indies, it will be necessary to make such an alteration of the present nominal rates of the dollar and the doubloon as will render the nominal proportions commensurate with the actual proportions.

As all existing contracts have reference to the over-rated gold coins, it will be proper to retain the present denomination of the doubloon, and to raise the present denomination of the dollar in the proportion of 15·36 to 16.

The effect of the alteration will be to give to 15·36 dollars the same current denomination as is now given to 1 doubloon, and to render 15·36 dollars and 1 doubloon equivalent tenders of payment for the same amount of nominal currency.

Her Majesty has been pleased to revoke the Order in Council made on the 23rd day of March, 1825, and by a new Order to approve a Proclamation declaring that in Her colonial possessions in the West Indies and America, 4s. 2d. and 64s. of British silver shall be deemed legal tenders for 1 dollar and 1 doubloon respectively. Hence, whatever may be the current denominations of the two coins in any of the colonies referred to in the Order, the same denominations will be applicable to 4s. 2d. and 64s. of British silver.

In those islands where 64 English shillings and one doubloon are at present conventionally regarded as equivalent tenders of payment, no other practical alteration will be made than to give a new denomination to the silver of Mexico and South America, on the principle and in the manner which I have above described.

I have, &c.

(*Circular.*)

Sir, Downing-street, September, 1838.

In obedience to the commands of Her Majesty in Council, I herewith transmit to you two Orders in Council, dated respectively the 7th and the 14th instant, with the Royal Proclamation to which the last of those Orders refers. The Order of the 7th instant revokes the Order in Council of the 23rd of March, 1825, so far as it relates to the West Indian and North American colonies. The Order of the 14th instant approves the Proclamation by which Her Majesty has been pleased to determine the proportionate rates at which the Spanish dollar and the doubloon are hereafter to pass current in the British West Indies.

In my accompanying circular despatch of this date I have stated, for your information, the principles by which Her Majesty's Government have been guided in the introduction of these changes in the current value of foreign coins in the West Indian colonies. The object of the present communication is to point out to you the measures which it will be your duty to adopt on receiving the Royal Orders and Proclamation.

I trust that when the principles and objects of this measure shall be distinctly understood, there will be no reason to apprehend any serious or extensive objection to it. On the other hand, the subject is one on which misapprehensions are so readily conceived and propagated, that it is necessary to be prepared for some popular delusion as to the possible effects of these changes in the colonial currency. You will observe, therefore, that Her Majesty in Council has been pleased to declare that, until actually promulgated by you, the Proclamation of the 14th instant shall not take effect within the colony under your government. It will be in your power, therefore, to defer the publication of it for some short interval, which you might advantageously employ in communicating with the principal merchants, landed proprietors, and other leading persons in the colony on the subject.

You will avail yourself of that opportunity of explaining the motives by which Her Majesty's Government has been guided, and for removing any erroneous impressions which may at first be formed respecting the character and tendency of this measure. The interval of delay cannot however, I apprehend, be much protracted; for as the Orders and Proclamation must appear in the public Gazette in this country, and will therefore be universally known, and as their official promulgation in any one of the colonies to which they apply will render the same course inevitable in all the rest, it cannot be deferred for more than a short time in any.

You will of course observe that the Royal Proclamation is framed with reference only to the sterling money of Great Britain. But as the pecuniary transactions of the West Indian colonies are all entered into with reference to the various local currencies or monies of account, the measure will be incomplete and comparatively inefficient, if the effect of the change in the relative values of the British and foreign coins should not be authoritatively stated in the terms of that conventional currency. But after the most careful inquiry, it has been found impracticable to ascertain the relation of current and sterling money throughout all the different West Indian colonies, with the exactness and precision which would be requisite, if the Royal Proclamation were so framed as to embrace that branch of the subject. I find that in the year 1825 the same difficulty existed. It was at that time overcome by delegating to the respective Governors the duty of proclaiming in the various colonies the rates at which the Spanish dollar should pass current in the different local monies of account. Instructions to that effect were conveyed by Earl Bathurst, in his circular despatch accompanying the Order in Council of March, 1825. In pursuance of those instructions, various proclamations have been issued for this purpose by the Governors, which proclamations are still in force. It is proposed to follow this precedent on the present occasion.

You will, therefore, upon promulgating the Royal Proclamation, publish a subsidiary proclamation, declaring what is the sum of the money of account in the colony under your government to which the British shilling, the dollar, and the doubloon, are respectively equivalent. Her Majesty does not delegate to you any discretionary authority for determining the relative values of these coins in the terms of the local currency, but merely confides to you the duty of expressing with accuracy in those terms the proportions established between them by the Royal Proclamation. The meaning will perhaps be rendered more clear by the following illustration. Let it be supposed that in the colony under your government the doubloon is equivalent in money of account to five pounds, six shillings, and eight pence (5l. 6s. 8d.). The consequence will be, that the dollar will be equivalent to six shillings, eleven pence, and one-third of a penny (6s. 11⅓d.) of the money of account, and that the British shilling will be equivalent to one shilling and eight pence (1s. 8d.) of the same money of account.

The accuracy of these statements is readily shown, by

exhibiting in the usual arithmetical form the proportions which subsist between the sums to which I have referred. For 6s. 11⅓d. : 5l. 6s. 8d. :: 4s. 2d. : 64s., and 1s. 8d. : 6s. 11½d. :: 1s. : 4s. 2d.

Or, if it be supposed that, in the colony under your government, the doubloon is equivalent in money of account to eight pounds (8l.), then, according to the same rule of proportion, the dollar and the British shilling will be equivalent to ten shillings and five pence (10s. 5d.), and two shillings and sixpence (2s. 6d.) respectively, of the same money of account.

The assumptions as to the value of the doubloon in the local money of account may not coincide with the fact in the case of any one colony. They are stated merely by way of hypothesis and illustration, and will serve to show the principle on which the proportionate value of the British shilling, the dollar, and the doubloon, may be calculated in each colony, for the purpose of promulgating in each the subsidiary proclamation by which the rules laid down by Her Majesty in Council will be expressed in the terms of the various local currencies. When you shall have issued any such proclamation, you will communicate it to me, in order that it may receive Her Majesty's ultimate sanction and confirmation

I have, &c.

At the Court at Windsor, the 7th day of September, 1838.

Present, The Queen's Most Excellent Majesty in Council.

Whereas by an Order of His late Majesty King George the Fourth, made with the advice of his Privy Council, and bearing date the 23rd of March, 1825, after reciting, amongst other things, that it had been represented to His Majesty at the Council Board, by the Lords Commissioners of His Majesty's Treasury, that they had given directions that His Majesty's troops serving in the several British colonies and possessions abroad should, in certain cases, be paid in British silver and copper money; and that, with a view of securing the circulation of such money in those colonies, it would be expedient that an Order in Council should be issued, declaring that in all those colonies where the Spanish dollar was then, either by law, fact, or practice, considered as a legal tender for the discharge of debts; or where the duties of the Government were rated or collected, or the individuals had a right to be paid in that description of coin, that a tender and payment of British silver money, to the amount of four shillings and four pence, should be considered as equivalent to the tender or payment of one Spanish dollar, and so in proportion for any greater or less amount of debt; his said late Majesty was pleased to approve of what was proposed in the said representation.

And whereas it is expedient that the said recited Order in Council should be revoked, so far as respects Her Majesty's colonies and possessions in America and the West Indies, be it, therefore, and it is hereby ordered, by the Queen's Most Excellent Majesty, by and with the advice of her Privy Council, that so far as respects Her Majesty's colonies and possessions in America, and in the West Indies, the said recited Order shall be, and the same is hereby rescinded.

And the Right Honourable Lord Glenelg, one of Her Majesty's Principal Secretaries of State, is to give the necessary directions herein accordingly.

(Signed)   C. C. GREVILLE.

AT THE COURT AT WINDSOR, the 14th day of September, 1838.

Present, The QUEEN'S MOST EXCELLENT MAJESTY in Council.

WHEREAS there was this day read at the Board, the draft of a Proclamation regulating the rate at which certain foreign coins are to pass current in Her Majesty's West India colonies: Her Majesty having taken the same into consideration, was pleased, by and with the advice of Her Privy Council, to approve thereof, and to order, as it is hereby ordered, that the said Proclamation do take effect and come into force, in each of Her Majesty's said colonies, upon, and from and after such day as shall be, for that purpose, limited by the Governor or officer administering the Government of each of the said colonies respectively, by any proclamations to be by them respectively, for that purpose, issued in each of such respective colonies.

And the Right Honourable Lord Glenelg, one of Her Majesty's Principal Secretaries of State, is to give the necessary directions for causing publication to be made hereof within Her Majesty's said colonies.

(Signed)   C. C. GREVILLE.

BY THE QUEEN, A PROCLAMATION.

WHEREAS the coin current in Our West India colonies, including Our province of British Guiana, consisting partly of the current coin of the United Kingdom, and partly of Spanish, Mexican, and Columbian gold coin, called doubloons, and of Spanish, Mexican, and Columbian silver coin, called dollars; and it is expedient that the rate at which the said doubloons and dollars shall circulate in Our said colonies should be ascertained and fixed. Now therefore We, by the advice of Our Privy

Council, have thought fit to declare and ordain, and by the advice aforesaid, We do hereby declare and ordain, that throughout the whole of Our said colonies the said doubloon shall circulate and be received in payment as being of the full value of sixty-four shillings sterling, current money of the United Kingdom, and the said dollar shall circulate and be received in payment as being of the full value of four shillings and two pence sterling, like current money of the United Kingdom. And in all payments to be made in any of Our said colonies, tender of payment in doubloons and dollars, or either of them, at the rate aforesaid, shall be deemed and taken to be a lawful tender, in the same manner as if such tender had been made in the current coin of the United Kingdom.

Given at Our Court at Windsor, this Fourteenth Day of September One Thousand Eight Hundred and Thirty-Eight, and in the Second Year of Our Reign.

God Save the Queen.

MAURITIUS.

(L. S.)

AT THE COURT AT WINDSOR, the 1st of February, 1843.

Present, The QUEEN'S MOST EXCELLENT MAJESTY in Council.

WHEREAS by an Order of His late Majesty King George the Fourth, made with the advice of his Privy Council, and bearing date the 23rd of March, 1825, after reciting, amongst other things, that it had been represented to His Majesty at the Council Board, by the Lords Commissioners of His Majesty's Treasury, that they had given directions that His Majesty's troops serving in the several British colonies and possessions abroad, should in certain cases be paid in British silver and copper money, and that with a view of securing the circulation of such money in those colonies, it would be expedient that an Order in Council should be issued declaring that in all those colonies where the Spanish dollar was then, either by law, fact, or practice, considered as a legal tender for the discharge of debts; or where the duties to the Government were rated or collected, or the individuals had a right to be paid in that description of coin, that a tender and payment of British silver money to the amount of 4s. 4d. should be considered as equivalent to the tender or payment of one Spanish dollar, and so in proportion for any greater or less amount of debt; His said late Majesty was pleased to approve of what was proposed in the said representation.

And whereas it is expedient that the said recited Order in Council should be revoked so far as respects Her Majesty's colony of Mauritius and its dependencies; be it therefore and it is hereby ordered by the Queen's Most Excellent Majesty, by and with the advice of her Privy Council, that so far as respects Her Majesty's said colony of the Mauritius and its dependencies, the said recited Order shall be and the same is hereby rescinded.

And the Lords Commissioners of Her Majesty's Treasury, and the Right Honourable Lord Stanley, one of Her Majesty's Principal Secretaries of State, are to give the necessary directions herein accordingly.

(Signed)   WILLIAM L. BATHURST.

A PROCLAMATION BY THE QUEEN.

WHEREAS the coin current in Our colony of the Mauritius and its dependencies consisting partly of the current coin of the United Kingdom, and partly of the gold and silver coin current in the territories of the East

India Company, or of gold and silver coin of Foreign States; and it is expedient that the rate at which the said gold and silver coin of the territories of the East India Company or of Foreign States shall circulate in Our said colony shall be ascertained and fixed.

Now therefore We, by the advice of Our Privy Council, have thought fit to declare and ordain, and by the advice aforesaid We do hereby declare and ordain that throughout Our said colony of the Mauritius and its dependencies the said gold coins shall circulate and be received in payment, as being of the full value and equivalent to current money of the United Kingdom, at the rates hereafter specified, that is to say—

The doubloon of Spain, Mexico, or the States of South America at the rate of 64s. sterling.

The gold mohur of the East India Company's territory, coined since the 1st day of September, 1835, at the rate of 29s. 2d. sterling.

The French gold piece of 20 francs, at the rate of 15s. 10d. sterling.

And the said silver coins shall circulate and be received in payment as being of the full value and equivalent to current money of the United Kingdom, at the following rates, that is to say,

The dollar of Spain, Mexico, or the South American States, at the rate of 4s. 2d. sterling.

The rupee of the East India Company's territory, coined since the 1st day of September, 1835, at the rate of 1s. 10d. sterling.

The French piece of five francs, or French pieces of one and two francs to the same amount (viz. five francs), at the rate of 3s. 10½d. sterling; provided always that the said French silver coins shall not be a legal tender in sums of less than five francs.

And in all payments to be made in Our said colony of

Mauritius or its dependencies tender of payment in the said coins or either of them, at the several respective rates aforesaid, shall be deemed and taken to be a lawful tender, in the same manner as if such tender had been made in the current coin of the United Kingdom.

(L. S.)

At the Court at Windsor, the 1st day of February, 1843.

Present, The Queen's Most Excellent Majesty in Council.

Whereas there was this day read at the Board the draft of a Proclamation regulating the rates at which certain foreign coins and coins of the East India Company's territories are to pass current in Her Majesty's colony of the Mauritius and its dependencies; Her Majesty having taken the same into consideration was pleased, by and with the advice of Her Privy Council, to approve thereof, and to order, and it is hereby ordered, that the said Proclamation do take effect and come into force in Her Majesty's said colony and the dependencies thereof, upon and from and after such day as shall be for that purpose limited by the Governor or officer administering the Government of the same, by a proclamation to be by him for that purpose issued.

And the Right Honourable Lord Stanley, one of Her Majesty's Principal Secretaries of State, is to give the requisite directions for causing publication to be made hereof in Her Majesty's said colony, and for the other purposes referred to herein.

(Signed)   C. Greville.

Extract from Treasury Minute of 7th March, 1845, *relating to the Currency at the Mauritius.*

" THE intention of Her Majesty's Proclamation and of the other measures the Governor was simultaneously directed to adopt, was to establish at the Mauritius, more effectually than had been done by the arrangements of 1825, an ascertained and settled standard of value, based upon and assimilated to the standard of the United Kingdom, which may also be considered as the legitimate standard for Her Majesty's colonial possessions; and at the same time, by legalizing the tender of certain foreign or Indian coins, to provide against scarcity of metallic circulating medium from want of ready access to supplies of British coins. Arrangements to this effect had already been very beneficially adopted in most of Her Majesty's colonial possessions, and the extension of them to the Mauritius had become urgently necessary as the only apparent means of preventing the recurrence of those difficulties and embarassments, as regarded the circulating medium, to which the inhabitants and the Government had been exposed.

" With these views, in addition to British coin, the currency and tender of coins of foreign states or of the East India Company's possessions has been legalized; but, to guard against any infringement of the integrity of the standard of value, this legalization has been effected with reference to the value of the several coins as compared with the British sovereign or pound sterling. As regarded gold coins, this comparative value would obviously be determined by their contents in pure gold; but, as regarded silver coins, reference could only properly be had for determining the comparative value, first, to the contents of the coins in pure silver, and, secondly, to the general marketable value of that silver in British sterling money.

" Independently of casual and temporary variations,

the relative value of pure silver to pure gold, as indicated by the transactions in the principal bullion markets of the world, has been for some years past about 15·7 of silver to 1 of gold, equivalent, as nearly as may be, to a money price of 5s. British sterling for the ounce of silver of British standard fineness. According to this price, the rates at which foreign or Indian silver coins should circulate and be a legal tender in the British colonies, have been fixed; and not with any reference to their value as compared with the silver coins of the United Kingdom.

" The fact of the British silver coins being in effect tokens, passing at nominal rates above their intrinsic value, would appear not to have been adverted to either by the President of the Mauritius Bank, or by the financial officers ; and the omission to advert to this fact has doubtless led to the erroneous conclusions at which those parties appear to have arrived, in regard to the propriety or probable effects of enhancing the value of the rupee.

" The circumstances, however, under which British silver coins and the silver coins of foreign states or of the East India Company are issued, and can be obtained for circulation in the colonies, are by no means analogous; inasmuch as, that while there is no limitation to the coinage and issue of the foreign or Indian coins, the British silver coins can only be procured to a limited amount by special orders for their preparation and issue at Her Majesty's Mint, and upon payment for them of their full nominal value; and they are not to be obtained from the Mint at the option of any party who may casually require them. Although, therefore, these coins are, as above stated, strictly speaking only tokens, and as such are a legal tender within the United Kingdom to a limited amount only, they are readily accepted in payment of sums much beyond that limit, and in all ordinary pecuniary transactions their nominal value is fully maintained.

" In the colonies the value of these coins is further established and maintained by their being made receivable at their nominal rates, without limitation of amount, in payment of all public duties, whether under imperial or colonial laws, and in exchange for all bills negotiated for the public service, and in all other public money transactions; and they are also generally available for remittance to any amouut to the mother country or to other colonies.

" In consideration of these circumstances, and of the ample security they afford for the realization at all times of the full nominal value of the coins, it has been found expedient that British silver coins at their nominal value should be a legalized tender in the colonies without limitation.

" If any inconvenience had been found to result from this arrangement, it would have been incumbent on Her Majesty's Government to place a limitation on the tender of these coins; but as they are not in request, unless in very peculiar cases, for purposes of foreign mercantile remittance, and are therefore less liable than other coins to be withdrawn from local circulation, they have been found to constitute a very useful and effective local currency, especially in distant and isolated colonies.

" The circumstances thus premised will evince to Sir W. Gomm and to the financial officers of his Government, that the rates at which foreign or Indian silver coins are to circulate, when legalized as a tender, in the colonies, can in no respect depend on any comparison of their intrinsic value with that of the silver coins of this country; but that those rates are to be determined with reference to the value of the coins as compared with British sterling money."

WEST COAST OF AFRICA.

(L. S.)

AT THE COURT AT BUCKINGHAM PALACE, the 10th June, 1843.

Present, The QUEEN'S MOST EXCELLENT MAJESTY in Council.

WHEREAS by an Order of His late Majesty King George the Fourth, made with the advice of his Privy Council, and bearing date the 23rd of March, 1825, after reciting amongst other things that it had been represented to His Majesty at the Council Board, by the Lords Commissioners of His Majesty's Treasury, that they had given directions that His Majesty's troops serving in the several British colonies and possessions abroad, should, in certain cases, be paid in British silver and copper money, and that with the view of securing the circulation of such money in those colonies, it would be expedient that an Order in Council should be issued, declaring that in all those colonies where the Spanish dollar was then, either by law, fact, or practice, considered as a legal tender for the discharge of debts; or where the duties to the Government were rated or collected, or the individuals had a right to be paid in that description of coin, that a tender and payment of British silver money to the amount of 4s. 4d. should be considered as equivalent to the tender and payment of one Spanish dollar, and so on in proportion for any greater or less amount of debt; his said late Majesty was pleased to approve of what was proposed in the said representation.

And whereas it is expedient that the said recited Order in Council should be revoked, so far as respects Her Majesty's colonies and possessions at Sierra Leone, the River Gambia, Cape Coast, and elsewhere on the western coast of the continent of Africa, and any dependencies thereon; be it therefore and it is hereby ordered by the Queen's Most Excellent Majesty, by and with the advice of Her Privy Council, that so far as respects Her Majesty's said colonies and possessions, the said recited Order shall be and the same is hereby rescinded.

And the Lords Commissioners of Her Majesty's Treasury, and the Right Honourable Lord Stanley, one of Her Majesty's Principal Secretaries of State, are to give the necessary directions herein accordingly.

(Signed) Wm. L. Bathurst.

A Proclamation by the Queen.

Whereas the coins current in Our colonies and possessions at Sierra Leone, the River Gambia, Cape Coast, and elsewhere on the western coast of the continent of Africa, consisting partly of the current coin of the United Kingdom, and partly of the gold and silver coins of foreign states; and it is expedient that the rates at which the said gold and silver coins of foreign states shall circulate in Our said colonies and possessions shall be ascertained and fixed: Now therefore We, by the advice of Our Privy Council, have thought fit to declare and ordain, and by the advice aforesaid We do hereby declare and ordain, that throughout Our said colonies and possessions at Sierra Leone, the River Gambia, Cape Coast, or elsewhere on the western coast of the continent of Africa, and the dependencies thereof, the said gold coins shall circulate and be received in payment, as being of the full value and equivalent to current money of the United Kingdom, at the rates hereafter specified; that is to say,

The doubloon of Spain, Mexico, or the States of South America, at the rate of 64s. sterling.

The French gold piece of 20 francs, at the rate of 15s. 10d. sterling.

And the said silver coins shall circulate and be received in payment, as being of the full value and equivalent to current money of the United Kingdom, at the following rates; that is to say,

The dollar of Spain, Mexico, or the South American States, at the rate of 4s. 2d. sterling.

The French piece of five francs, at the rate of 3s. 10½d. sterling.

And in all payments to be made in Our said colonies and possessions above mentioned, tender of payment in the said coins, or either of them, at the several respective rates aforesaid, shall be deemed and taken to be a lawful tender, in the same manner as if such tender had been made in the current coin of the United Kingdom.

(L. S.) ————————————

AT THE COURT AT BUCKINGHAM PALACE, the 10th of June, 1843.

Present, The QUEEN'S MOST EXCELLENT MAJESTY in Council.

WHEREAS there was this day read at the Board the draft of a Proclamation regulating the rates at which certain foreign coins are to pass current in Her Majesty's colonies and possessions in Sierra Leone, the River Gambia, Cape Coast, or elsewhere on the western coast of the continent of Africa, and their dependencies ; Her Majesty having taken the same into consideration, was pleased, by and with the advice of Her Privy Council, to approve thereof, and to order, and it is hereby ordered, that the said Proclamation do take effect and come into force in Her Majesty's said colonies and possessions, upon and from and after such day as shall be for that purpose limited by the Governor or officer administering the

Government of the colony of Sierra Leone, by a proclamation or proclamations to be by him for that purpose issued.

And the Lords Commissioners of Her Majesty's Treasury, and the Right Honourable Lord Stanley, one of Her Majesty's Principal Secretaries of State, are to give the requisite directions for causing publication to be made hereof in Her Majesty's said colonies and possessions, and for the other purposes referred to therein accordingly.

(Signed)   WM. L. BATHURST.

ST. HELENA.

(L. S.)

AT THE COURT AT BUCKINGHAM PALACE, the 15th of July, 1843.

Present, The QUEEN'S MOST EXCELLENT MAJESTY in Council.

WHEREAS it hath been represented to Her Majesty, that under and by virtue of a Proclamation issued by the Governor of St. Helena, bearing date the 29th day of February, 1836, the under-mentioned foreign gold and silver coins were declared to be current in that island, at the rates with reference to the current sterling money of the United Kingdom hereinafter specified, viz. :—

GOLD COINS.

	£.	s.	d.
Doubloons	3	6	0
Joes (Portuguese).	1	13	3
Bengal mohurs (having the star) .	1	13	3
Bombay and all other mohurs .	1	10	2
Moidores	1	6	0
Napoleons and Louis d'or. . .	0	15	7
10-Guilder pieces	0	15	7
Venetians	0	9	4
Star pagodas	0	7	3
Porto Nova Pagodas	0	5	6

Silver Coins.

	£.	s.	d.
Ducatoons	0	5	4
3-Guilder pieces	0	4	8
Dollars, Spanish and South American	0	4	4
Dollars, United States	0	4	4
Half-star pagodas	0	3	8
Colonial pieces (English coined)	0	2	4
Sicca rupees, (having the star)	0	2	1
Bombay and all other rupees	0	1	11
Dutch guilders	0	1	6
5-Franc piece	0	4	0
2-Franc piece	0	1	8
1-Franc piece	0	0	10

And whereas it is expedient that the said Proclamation, so far as regards the future currency or circulation of the said coins, and the sterling rates assigned thereto, should be revoked and annulled. Be it therefore and it is hereby ordered by the Queen's Most Excellent Majesty, by and with the advice of Her Privy Council, that from and after the dates of the receipt and publication of these presents in the said island of Saint Helena, the said Proclamation shall be revoked and annulled accordingly.

And the Lords Commissioners of Her Majesty's Treasury and the Right Honourable Lord Stanley, one of Her Majesty's Principal Secretaries of State, are to give the necessary directions herein accordingly.

(Signed)   WM. L. BATHURST.

A Proclamation by the Queen.

WHEREAS the coin current in Our island of St. Helena, consisting partly of the current coin of the United Kingdom, and partly of gold and silver coin of foreign states, and it is expedient that the rate at which any such foreign gold or silver coins shall circulate, and be deemed and taken as a legal tender of payment in our said island, shall be ascertained and fixed: Now, therefore, We, by the advice of Our Privy Council, have thought fit to declare and ordain, and by the advice aforesaid We do hereby declare and ordain, that throughout Our said island of St. Helena the gold doubloon of Spain, Mexico, or the states of South America, shall circulate and be received in payment as being of the full value of 64 shillings sterling current money of the United Kingdom; and the silver dollar of Spain, Mexico, or the South American States, shall circulate and be received in payment as being of the full value of 4s. 2d. sterling, like current money of the United Kingdom.

And in all payments to be made in our said island tender of payment in doubloons and dollars, of either of them, at the respective rates aforesaid, shall be deemed and taken to be a lawful tender in the same manner as if such tender had been made in the current coin of the United Kingdom.

(L.S.)

AT THE COURT AT BUCKINGHAM PALACE, the 15th of July, 1843.

Present, The QUEEN'S MOST EXCELLENT MAJESTY in Council.

WHEREAS there was this day read at the Board the draft of a Proclamation regulating the rates at which certain foreign coins are to pass current in Her Majesty's island of St. Helena; Her Majesty having taken the same into consideration, was pleased, by and with the advice of Her Privy Council, to approve thereof, and to order, and it is hereby ordered, that the said Proclamation do take effect and come into force in Her Majesty's said island upon and from and after such day as shall be for that purpose limited by the Governor or officer administering the Government of the same by a Proclamation to be by him for that purpose issued.

And the Lords Commissioners of Her Majesty's Treasury, and the Right Honourable Lord Stanley, one of Her Majesty's Principal Secretaries of State, are to give the requisite directions for causing publication to be made hereof in Her Majesty's said island, and for the other purposes referred to herein.

(Signed) WM. L. BATHURST.

MALTA.

(L.S.)

AT THE COURT AT BUCKINGHAM PALACE, the 4th of March, 1844.

Present, The QUEEN'S MOST EXCELLENT MAJESTY in Council.

WHEREAS by an Order of His late Majesty King George the Fourth, made with the advice of his Privy Council, and bearing date the 23rd of March, 1825, after reciting amongst other things that it had been represented to His Majesty at the Council Board, by the Lords Commissioners of His Majesty's Treasury, that they had given directions that His Majesty's troops serving in the several British colonies and possessions abroad, should in certain cases be paid in British silver and copper money, and that with the view of securing the circulation of such money in those colonies, it would be expedient that an Order in Council should be issued, declaring that in all those colonies where the Spanish dollar was then, either by law, fact, or practice, considered as a legal tender for the discharge of debts; or where the duties to the Government were rated or collected, or the individuals had a right to pay in that description of coin, that a tender and payment of British silver money, to the amount of 4s. 4d., should be considered as equivalent to the tender or payment of one Spanish dollar, and so in proportion for any greater or less amount of debt; and also that British copper money should be made a legal tender in all the British colonies, for its due and proper proportions of British silver money as by law established in Great Britain, but that no person should be compelled to take more than 12d. in copper money at one payment : his said late Majesty was pleased to approve of what was proposed in the said representation.

And whereas it is expedient that the said Order in Council should be revoked so far as respects Her Majesty's colony of Malta and its dependencies, save and except that part of it which relates to the tender and payment of British copper money; be it therefore and it is hereby ordered by the Queen's Most Excellent Majesty, by and with the advice of Her Privy Council, that so far as respects Her Majesty's said colony of Malta and its dependencies, the said recited Order, save and except as it regards the tender of British copper money, shall be and the same is hereby rescinded.

And whereas, on the 11th day of October, in the year 1825, Lieutenant-General Sir Manley Power, Knight Commander of the Most Honourable Military Order of the Bath, and Lieutenant-Governor administering the Government of the island of Malta and its dependencies, did cause to be published in the said island, the said Order made by His late Majesty King George the Fourth, by and with the advice of his Privy Council, on the 23rd of March 1825, relating to the circulation and tender of British silver and copper money in the colonies, and did thereupon further cause to be published a Proclamation in the words following; that is to say,

" His Honour the Lieutenant-Governor having received, for his information and guidance, the foregoing

Order of His Majesty in Council from the Right Honourable the Earl of Bathurst, one of His Majesty's Principal
Secretaries of State, is pleased to order and direct as
follows:

"That from the 25th day of December next inclusive,
the several provisions of the said Order of His Majesty in
Council shall be strictly observed and enforced, so far as
they are applicable to this island and its dependencies;
and debts and engagements for the payment of money
shall be dischargable in British silver money, or in
Spanish pillar dollars, at the rate of 4s. 4d. each, at the
option of the debtor.

"That from the said date, British copper money shall
be within these possessions a legal tender for its due and
proper proportions of British silver money as by law
established in Great Britain; provided that no person be
compelled to take more than 12d. in copper money at any
one payment.

"That from the same date shall stand repealed
the Proclamation of the 10th of June, 1824, fixing
the current value in Maltese currency of the Spanish
dollar; which thenceforth shall pass current in exchange
with Maltese currency for the same amount in that currency as 4s. 4d. of the British silver money : the British
metallic currency continuing to be equivalent in reference
to, and in exchange with, Maltese currency at the rates
specified in the Proclamation of the 9th June last.

"That from the said 25th day of December next
inclusive, the Spanish dollar will be issued, in all payments on Government account, at the said rate of 4s. 4d.;
and all dues to the Crown shall be paid either in British
silver money, or in Spanish dollars at the rate of 4s. 4d.
each, or in Maltese currency (at the rates specified in the
Proclamation above mentioned of the 9th June last),
at the option of the person paying, according to the

printed schedules put up in the respective public offices. All Government accounts, however, will, from and after the said date, be kept and rendered exclusively in British money."

And whereas, on the 22nd day of November, in the year 1825, the said Lieutenant-Governor administering the Government of the Island of Malta did cause to be published in the said island, a minute or notification in the following words; that is to say,

"His Honour the Lieutenant-Governor, in adverting to the Proclamation of the 11th October last, is pleased to notify, for general information, that the Sicilian dollar will be received after the 25th December next by the Government Treasury, and paid away by it at the same rate as at present."

And whereas, on the 27th day of May, 1834, Major-General the Honourable Frederick Cavendish Ponsonby, Lieutenant-Governor administering the Government of the Island of Malta and its dependencies, caused to be published in the said island a proclamation in the words following; that is to say,

"Whereas His Majesty's Government has deemed it expedient that the military chests in the colonies shall be supplied with dollars of the South American States, as hereinafter more particularly described; and whereas, it is therefore necessary to provide for the free circulation within these islands of the coins above mentioned, his Excellency the Lieutenant-Governor is hereby pleased to order and direct,

"1. That, from and after the date hereof, the dollar of the following South American States, namely, Mexico, Peru, Bolivia, Chili, and Rio Plata, shall pass current within these islands, at the rate of 4s. 4d. British sterling money, being the same rate at which the Spanish pillar dollar is now current in these possessions.

"2. That, from the said date, the South American dollars above mentioned will be received and issued by the Treasury of this island, and by all Government agents and authorities, at the rate in British sterling specified in the preceding article."

And whereas, on the 1st day of September, in the year 1838, a " Government notice," published by the command of the Governor of Malta, stating that, " Whereas various small silver coins of certain foreign states," which had " by general sufference, though not otherwise legally, passed current, at fractional rates respectively corresponding with the value of the Maltese or current dollar of 30 tari, his Excellency the Governor has been pleased to direct that no such foreign silver coins below the value of current dollars, except only certain half-dollar pieces (which will be taken as heretofore), will be received at the Treasury of the island, or by any agent or public officer of the Government, after the 10th day of the present month."

And whereas it is expedient that the said hereinbefore recited proclamations of officers administering the Government of Malta, of the 11th day of October, 1825, and of the 27th day of May, 1834, and likewise the said recited notification of the 22nd day of November, 1825, and also the Government notice of the 1st day of September, 1838, so far as the circulation or tender of half-dollar pieces might be authorized thereby, should be revoked; be it therefore, and it is hereby further ordered, by the Queen's Most Excellent Majesty, by and with the advice of Her Privy Council, that from and after the date of the publication of these presents, in the Island of Malta, by the Governor or officer administering the Government thereof, the said proclamations, notification, and Government notice, shall be, and the same are hereby revoked and rescinded.

And whereas, on the 9th day of June, in the year 1825, the said Lieutenant-General Sir Manley Power, Lieutenant-Governor administering the Government of the Island of Malta and its dependencies, caused to be published in the said island a proclamation, in the words and figures following ; that is to say,

"His Honour the Lieutenant-Governor is pleased to enact and declare, that from and after the 24th instant the British silver and copper coins hereinafter enumerated shall pass current in the Island of Malta and its dependencies, at the following rates respectively of Maltese money, viz. :—

SILVER.

	Scudi.	Tari.	Grains.	Grains.
The crown or 5-shilling piece .	3	0	0 or	720
The half-crown 2s. 6d. ditto .	1	6	0 ,,	360
The shilling	0	7	4 ,,	144
The sixpence	0	3	12 ,,	72

COPPER.

The penny	12
The halfpenny	6
The farthing	3

" In all payments to Government, the above-mentioned British coins will be received at the Treasury and all other public offices of the Government, at the rates specified in Maltese currency, and issued in the same manner.

"His Honour is pleased further to notify that the measure above stated is preparatory to the general introduction of the British metallic currency, as the circulating medium in these possessions."

And whereas, on the 6th day of March, in the year 1826, Major-General Alexander Woodford, as Lieutenant-Governor administering the Government of the Island of Malta and its dependencies, caused to be published in the

said island a proclamation, in the words and figures following ; that is to say,

" His Honour the Lieutenant-Governor, with reference
to the proclamation of the 9th of June, 1825 (No. XIV.)
is pleased to order and direct that the British gold coins,
called sovereigns and half-sovereigns, shall hereafter pass
current in these islands for their relative value of 20*s.*
and 10*s.* sterling each respectively."

And whereas, on the 3rd day of November, in the year
1827, the said Major-General the Honourable Frederick
Cavendish Ponsonby, Lieutenant-Governor administering
the Government of the Island of Malta and its dependencies, caused to be published in the said island a proclamation in the words following ; that is to say,

" Whereas, by the Proclamation No. XIV., dated the
9th June, 1825, the intention of His Majesty's Government generally to introduce the British metallic currency
as the circulating medium in these possessions was avowed
and declared, and with that view the British silver and
copper coins, viz., crowns, half-crowns, shillings, and sixpences, pence, half-pence, and farthings, were ordained to
be here current at the rates respectively of Maltese money
therein mentioned ; and whereas His Majesty deeming
it expedient that a copper coin of a less value than the
British farthing (now current at the rate of three Malta
grains each) should be provided for the accommodation
of this population, was graciously pleased to order that
certain pieces of copper money should be coined in England, which should be called 'British grains,' every such
piece having for the obverse impression His Majesty's
effigy, with the inscription 'Georgius IV. Dei Gratia'
and the date of the year, and for the reverse the figure
of Britannia, represented seated holding a trident in her
left hand, with the emblems of the United Kingdom
underneath the figure, and with the inscription 'Britan-

niar : Rex Fid : Def: ' and whereas the said coin is now arrived and at the disposal of Government, the Lieut.-Governor enacts and declares, that the British grains above described shall, from and after the date of this proclamation, pass and be received, within the island of Malta and its dependencies, as current and lawful money of Great Britain, every such grain piece as of the value of one grain of Malta money, and in relation to and exchange for other British copper coin as follows, viz. :—

> 12 for one penny piece ;
> 6 for one halfpenny ;
> 3 for one farthing ;

at which said rates the British grain will henceforth be paid and received by the Treasury, and other officers of the Government."

And whereas, on the 6th day of November, in the year 1827, the said Lieutenant-Governor, the Honourable Frederick Cavendish Ponsonby, caused to be published in the said island of Malta a further proclamation, stating that,

"Whereas a new copper coinage, fully adequate and well adapted to the wants and accommodation of the people, has now, through the paternal care of His Majesty's Government, been provided for circulation, and established as current in these possessions, his Excellency the Lieutenant-Governor is pleased to enact and ordain :

"1. That from and after the 20th of November then instant, no copper money, except the British penny, halfpenny, farthing and grain pieces, shall pass or be received as the lawful currency of the Island of Malta and its dependencies.

"2. That, consequently, from and after the said date the Malta copper money, namely, the four, two, and one tari pieces, and the ten, five, and one grain pieces, shall cease to be current, and shall no longer be considered as coins of any value."

And further providing for the exchange of the said Malta copper money for other current money of the island.

And whereas, it is expedient that the provisions and directions contained in the said recited proclamations of the 9th day of June, 1825, of the 6th day of March, 1826, of the 3rd and 6th days of November, 1827, should be approved and confirmed; be it therefore, and it is hereby further ordered, by the Queen's Most Excellent Majesty, oy and with the advice of Her Privy Council, that the same shall be and are hereby approved and confirmed accordingly. Provided always, and it is hereby further ordered and declared, that all acts, matters, and things heretofore done, under or by virtue of the said proclama-tions or notices now confirmed, or under or by virtue of the said proclamations or notices which are hereby revoked and rescinded, or any or either of them, shall be and remain valid and effectual to all intents and purposes, as if the said proclamations had been issued or confirmed by Her Majesty or Her Royal predecessors.

And the Lords Commissioners of Her Majesty's Trea-sury, and the Right Honourable Lord Stanley, one of Her Majesty's Principal Secretaries of State, are to give the necessary directions herein accordingly.

(Signed)   WILLIAM L. BATHURST.

A PROCLAMATION BY THE QUEEN.

WHEREAS the coins current in Our Island of Malta and its dependencies consist partly of the current coin of the United Kingdom, and partly of Spanish, Mexican, and Columbian silver coins called dollars, and it is expedient

that the rate at which the said dollars shall circulate in
Our said colony shall be correctly ascertained and fixed:
Now therefore We, by the advice of Our Privy Council,
have thought fit to declare and ordain, and by the advice
aforesaid do hereby declare and ordain, that throughout
Our said Island of Malta and its dependencies, the dollar
of Spain, Mexico, or the South American States, shall circulate and be received in payment as being of the full
value and equivalent to 4s. 2d. sterling money of the
United Kingdom. And in all payments to be made in
Our said Island and its dependencies, tender or payment
in the said coins, at the rate aforesaid, shall be deemed
and taken to be a lawful tender, in the same manner as if
such tender had been made in the current coin of the
United Kingdom.

(L. S.)

AT THE COURT AT BUCKINGHAM PALACE, the 4th of
March, 1844.

Present, The QUEEN'S MOST EXCELLENT MAJESTY in
Council.

WHEREAS there was this day read at the Board the
draft of a Proclamation, regulating the rate at which certain foreign coins are to pass current in Her Majesty's
Island of Malta and its dependencies; Her Majesty
having taken the same into consideration, was pleased, by
and with the advice of Her Privy Council, to approve
thereof, and to order, and it is hereby ordered, that the
said Proclamation do take effect and come into force in
Her Majesty's said island and the dependencies thereof,
from and after such day as shall be for that purpose
limited by the Governor or officer administering the
Government of the same by a proclamation to be by him
for that purpose issued.

And the Lords Commissioners of Her Majesty's Treasury, and the Right Honourable Lord Stanley, one of Her Majesty's Principal Secretaries of State, are to give requisite directions for causing publication to be made hereof in Her Majesty's said island, and for other purposes referred to therein.

(Signed)   Wm. L. Bathurst.

GIBRALTAR.

(L. S.)

At the Court at Buckingham Palace, the 23rd of May, 1844.

Present, The Queen's Most Excellent Majesty in Council.

Whereas by an Order of His late Majesty King George the Fourth, made with the advice of his Privy Council, and bearing date the 23rd March, 1825, after reciting amongst other things, that it had been represented to His Majesty at the Council Board, by the Lords Commissioners of His Majesty's Treasury, that they had given directions that His Majesty's troops serving in the several British colonies and possessions abroad should in certain cases be paid in British silver and copper money, and that with the view of securing the circulation of such money in those colonies, it would be expedient that an Order in Council should be issued, declaring that in all those colonies where the Spanish dollar was then, either by law, fact, or practice, considered as a legal tender for the discharge of debts, or where the duties of the Government were rated or collected, or the individuals had a right to be paid in that description of coin, that a tender and payment of British silver money to the amount of 4s. 4d. should be considered as equivalent to the tender and payment of one Spanish dollar, and so on in proportion for any greater or less amount of debt; his said late Majesty was pleased to approve of what was proposed in the said representation.

And whereas it is expedient that the said recited Order in Council should be revoked so far as respects Her Majesty's garrison and territory of Gibraltar, be it therefore, and it is hereby ordered by the QUEEN's Most Excellent Majesty, by and with the advice of Her Privy Council, that so far as respects Her Majesty's said garrison and territory the said recited Order shall be, and the same is hereby rescinded.

And the Lords Commissioners of Her Majesty's Treasury, and the Right Honourable Lord Stanley, one of Her Majesty's Principal Secretaries of State, are to give the necessary directions herein accordingly.

(Signed)   WM. L. BATHURST.

PROCLAMATION BY THE QUEEN.

WHEREAS the coins current within Our garrison and territory of Gibraltar, consisting partly of the current coin of the United Kingdom, and partly of gold, silver, and copper coins of Spain, or of the South American States, and it is expedient that the rates at which the said Spanish or other foreign coins shall circulate within Our said garrison and territory shall be ascertained and fixed : Now therefore, We, by the advice of Our Privy Council, have thought fit to declare and ordain, and by the advice aforesaid We do hereby declare and ordain, that within and throughout Our said garrison and territory of Gibraltar, the said coins shall circulate and be received in payment as being of the full value, and equivalent to current money of the United Kingdom, at the rates hereafter specified ; that is to say,

The gold doubloon of Spain, Mexico, or the South American States, at the rate of 66s. 8d. sterling.

The gold or silver dollar of Spain, or the dollar of Mexico or the South American States, at the rate of 4s. 2d. sterling.

And We do further ordain and declare, that the copper coin denominated the quarto shall pass current and be received in payment as of the value and equivalent to the one hundred and ninety-second part of the said dollar; provided always, that no person shall be compelled to receive at any one payment more than forty-eight of the said quartos.

And in all payments to be made within Our said garrison and territory above mentioned, tenders of payment in the said coins or either of them at the several respective rates, but, as regards quartos, subject to the limitation as to amount as aforesaid, shall be deemed and taken to be a legal tender in the same manner as if such tender had been made in the current coin of the United Kingdom.

(L. S.)

AT THE COURT AT WINDSOR, the 3rd September, 1844.

Present, The QUEEN'S MOST EXCELLENT MAJESTY in Council.

WHEREAS there was this day read at the Board the draft of a Proclamation regulating the rates at which certain foreign coins are to pass current within Her Majesty's garrison and territory of Gibraltar; Her Majesty having taken the same into consideration was pleased, by and with the advice of Her Privy Council, to approve thereof, and to order, and it is hereby ordered, that the said Proclamation do take effect and come into force in Her Majesty's said garrison and territory, upon and from and after such day as shall be for that purpose limited by the Governor or officer administering the government of the same, by a proclamation to be by him for that purpose issued.

And the Right Honourable the Lords Commissioners

of Her Majesty's Treasury, and the Right Honourable Lord Stanley, one of Her Majesty's Principal Secretaries of State, are to give the requisite directions for causing publication to be made hereof in Her Majesty's said garrison and territory, and for the other purposes referred to herein accordingly.

(Signed)   C. GREVILLE.

A PROCLAMATION BY THE QUEEN.

WHEREAS by Our Proclamation for ascertaining and fixing the rates at which certain Spanish and other foreign coins shall circulate and be a lawful tender within Our garrison and territory of Gibraltar, it was among other things declared and ordained that the gold doubloon of Spain, Mexico, or the South American States should circulate and be received in payment as being of the full value and equivalent to 66s. 8d. of the current money of the United Kingdom. And whereas it hath been represented unto us by the Lords Commissioners of Our Treasury, that it is expedient that the directions thereby given, and the value therein set forth, should be applicable to the doubloon of Spain only. Now, therefore, We, by the advice of our Privy Council, have thought fit further to declare and ordain, and by the advice aforesaid We do hereby declare and ordain accordingly, that, so far as regards the circulation and tender of doubloons of Mexico or of the South American States, the directions given by Our said Proclamation shall be revoked and annulled.

(L. S.)

AT THE COURT AT BUCKINGHAM PALACE, the 26th April, 1845.

Present, The QUEEN'S MOST EXCELLENT MAJESTY in Council.

WHEREAS there was this day read at the Board the draft of a Proclamation revoking so much of a Proclamation for regulating the rates at which certain foreign coins are to pass current within Her Majesty's garrison and territory of Gibraltar, as relates to the circulation and lawful tender of doubloons of Mexico and of the South American States. Her Majesty, having taken the same into consideration, was pleased, by and with the advice of Her Privy Council, to approve thereof, and to order, and it is hereby ordered, that this Proclamation do take effect and come into force upon and from and after the promulgation thereof in Her Majesty's said garrison and territory by the Governor or officer administering the Government of the same.

And the Right Honourable the Lords Commissioners of Her Majesty's Treasury, and the ʀRight Honourable Lord Stanley, one of Her Majesty's Principal Secretaries of State, are to give the requisite directions herein accordingly.

(Signed)   WM. L. BATHURST.

HONG KONG.

AT THE COURT AT WINDSOR, the 28th November, 1844.

Present, The QUEEN'S MOST EXCELLENT MAJESTY in Council.

WHEREAS there was this day read at the Board the draft of a Proclamation respecting the rates at which certain foreign coins and coins of the East India Company's territories are to pass current in Her Majesty's colony of Hong Kong and its dependencies, and further relating to the standard of value and tender of payment within the said colony ; Her Majesty having taken the same into consideration, was pleased, by and with the advice of Her Privy Council, to approve thereof, and to order, and it is hereby ordered, that the said Proclamation do take effect and come into force from the date of the publication thereof in Her Majesty's said island of Hong Kong, by the Governor of the same.

And the Lords Commissioners of Her Majesty's Treasury, and the Right Honourable Lord Stanley, one of Her Majesty's Principal Secretaries of State, are to give the requisite directions for causing publication of the said Proclamation to be made in Her Majesty's said colony, and for the other several purposes referred to therein.

(Signed)   WM. L. BATHURST.

BY THE QUEEN, A PROCLAMATION.

WHEREAS, on the 29th day of March, 1842, a Proclamation was issued at Hong Kong by Sir Henry Pottinger, Baronet, Our Plenipotentiary and Chief Superintendent of the Trade of British Subjects in China, in the terms following, that is to say,—

" With reference to the desirable object of preventing disputes, and laying down some defined system regarding the circulating medium in this settlement, His Excellency Sir Henry Pottinger, Bart., Her Majesty's Plenipotentiary and Chief Superintendent of the Trade of British Subjects in China, is pleased to promulgate the following brief rules, which are to be considered applicable to all common bazaar purchases, and barter, hire, &c. &c., but not to interfere with, or affect what may be termed mercantile transactions, and are to be in force on the Island of Hong Kong, pending the gracious pleasure of Her Majesty the Queen of Great Britain.

" 1st. The following coins are to be deemed legal tenders:—Spanish, Mexican, and other dollars, and their component parts, Company's rupees and their component parts, ' cash,' or the copper coin current in China.

" 2nd. Dollars of whatever denomination or device, and whether whole or chopped, are to circulate at par with reference to each other, always providing that they be of the proper weight and standard.

" 3rd. Two and one quarter Company's rupees shall be considered equal to one dollar.

" One rupee and two annas (or half a quarter) equal to half a dollar, and three-quarters of a rupee (or 12 annas) equal to one quarter of a dollar.

" 4th. Twelve hundred cash (1200) copper coin shall be equal to one dollar.

" Six hundred (600) to half a dollar.

" Three hundred (300) to a quarter of a dollar.

" Five hundred and thirty-three (533) to one Company's rupee.

" Two hundred and sixty-six (266) to half a rupee.

" One hundred and thirty-three (133) to one quarter of a rupee.

" 5th. Any other coins, whether British or foreign, not enumerated in the preceding rules, are not to be deemed a legal tender, but they can, of course, be sold or otherwise bartered in the bazaar, according to their intrinsic value.

" 6th. Cash copper coin, at the rate laid down in the 4th rule, will be sold to any individual requiring it, in sums of not less than 50 dollars, on application to the Treasurer and Secretary to Her Britannic Majesty's Superintendent of Trade.

" God Save the Queen."

And whereas, on the 27th day of April, 1842, a further Proclamation was issued by Our said Plenipotentiary and Chief Superintendent of the Trade of British Subjects in China, in the terms following ;

That is to say,

" The letter, of which a copy is hereunto annexed, having been addressed to me by the mercantile firms who have signed it, on behalf of themselves and others, I do hereby direct and proclaim, in conformity with their application, that, pending the gracious pleasure of the Queen of England, the Mexican and other republican dollars shall be taken as, and considered to be, the standard, in all Government and mercantile transactions, at Hong Kong and other places in China in the occupation of Her Majesty's forces, unless at the time of such transactions taking place it should be expressly specified to the contrary.

" And I do further announce, that the present Proclamation is not to be taken in any way or shape as affecting the provisions of the one which I promulgated on the 29th day of last month, relative to the circulating medium on the island of Hong Kong.

" *God Save the Queen.*"

And whereas, by Our Letters Patent, bearing date the 5th day of April, in the sixth year of Our reign, We did erect and constitute Our island of Hong Kong and its dependencies into a separate colony, to be known and designated as the colony of Hong Kong. And by Our instructions to Our Governor of the said colony, We did then direct and ordain that he should not propose or assent to any legislative ordinance whatever, whereby any " bills of credit or any other paper currency, or any coin, save only the legal coin of the realm, may be made or declared to be a legal tender without special permission from Us in that behalf first obtained."

And whereas it hath been represented to Us, by the Lords Commissioners of Our Treasury, that doubts have arisen with reference to the terms of the said hereinbefore recited Proclamations of the 29th day of March and the 27th day of April, 1842, respecting the legal sufficiency of tenders of payment within Our said island and its dependencies in British coins; and it is expedient that such doubts should be removed, and that the regulations regarding standard of value and tenders of payment within Our said island should be assimilated to those of Our other possessions abroad.

Now, therefore, We, by the advice of Our Privy Council, have thought fit to declare and ordain, and, by the advice aforesaid, We do hereby declare and ordain, that from and after the date of the publication in the said island of Hong Kong of this Our Proclamation, the said hereinbefore recited Proclamations issued on the 29th day of March and 27th day of April, in the year 1842, as aforesaid, shall be revoked and annulled.

And We do further declare and ordain, that from and after the date of the publication, as aforesaid, of this Our Proclamation, the several coins hereinafter specified, being perfect coins, and of full and proper weight and value, shall, in like manner as the gold, silver, and copper coins of the United Kingdom, be and constitute a legal tender of payment within Our said island of Hong Kong and its dependencies, at the several respective rates, and as equivalent to the values undermentioned :

That is to say,

The gold mohur of the East India Company's territory, coined since the 1st day of September, 1835, at the rate of 29s. 2d. sterling money of the United Kingdom.

The dollar of Spain, Mexico, or the South American States, at the rate of 4s. 2d. sterling.

The rupee of the East India Company's territory,

coined since the 1st day of September, 1835, at the rate of 1s. 10d. sterling ; and the half rupee, quarter rupee, and eighth of rupee pieces, in proportion.

The cash, or copper coin, current in China, at the rate of 288 cash for 1s. sterling.

And we do hereby further declare and ordain, that tenders of payment in the said coins, being, as aforesaid, perfect coins, and of full and proper weight and value, as well as in the gold, silver, or copper coins of the United Kingdom, or any or either of them, according to the several relative rates and values hereinbefore specified, shall be deemed and taken within Our said Island of Hong Kong and its dependencies, to be a sufficient and lawful tender, in satisfaction and discharge of all debts, contracts, and engagements whatsoever for the payment of money ; provided always nevertheless, and We do further ordain and declare, that nothing herein contained shall be deemed or taken to render it compulsory on any person to accept at any one payment a larger amount in silver coins of the United Kingdom of lower denomination than 1s., or in the half-quarter or eighth rupee pieces hereinbefore mentioned, than the equivalent to 20s. sterling money, or a larger amount in copper coins of the United Kingdom, or in the Chinese copper coins before mentioned, than the equivalent to 1s. of sterling money.

BANKING COMPANIES IN THE COLONIES.

(*Circular.*)

Sir,   Downing-street, 30th May, 1846.

On the 4th of May, 1840, Lord J. Russell transmitted to you a Copy of Certain Regulations, the observance of which, in all Charters or Legislative Enactments relating to the Incorporation of Banking Companies in the Colonies, Her Majesty's Government then considered of much importance.

The Correspondence which has since taken place on subjects of this nature, and the arrangements adopted by Parliament in regard to Banks of Issue in the United Kingdom, appear to her Majesty's Government to have rendered necessary some modification of those Regulations, with a view to bring them into exact accordance with the principles on these subjects established in this Country. I accordingly transmit to you herewith a series of Regulations, revised with that object, to be substituted for those of May, 1840.

These Regulations are forwarded to you, not, of course, as inflexible rules to be in all cases insisted on, but as embodying the general principles to be observed in the preparation of Colonial Acts for the Incorporation of Banking Companies; and Her Majesty's Government consider a compliance with all the more material conditions and restrictions as of much importance to the security of the Communities in which such Banks may be established, and more especially to the poorer classes of such Communities. I must, therefore, desire you to take care, that in any Ordinances or Bills introduced into the Legislative Council of the Colony under your Government, for the Incorporation of Banking Companies, these conditions and restrictions be inserted.

I have the honour to be, Sir,

Your most obedient Servant,

Regulations and Conditions for the Observance of which Provision should be made in Charters or Legislative Enactments relating to the Incorporation of Banking Companies in the Colonies.

1st.—The Amount of the Capital of the Company and Number of Shares to be determined; and the whole of such determined amount to be subscribed for within a limited period, not exceeding Eighteen Months from the date of the Charter or Act of Incorporation.

2nd.—Shareholders to be declared a Body Corporate, with common seal and perpetual succession, and other usual corporate powers; and with any requisite proviso that judgment against the Corporation shall attach to all additional liability of the Shareholders, as well as to paid-up Capital and other property of the Company.

3rd.—Provision to be made, either by Recital and Confirmation of any Deed of Settlement in these respects or otherwise, for the due Management of the Company's Affairs by Appointment of Directors, and so forth, so far as shall seem necessary for the security of the Public.

4th.—No by-law of the Company to be repugnant to the conditions of the Charter or Act of Incorporation, or to the Laws of any Colony in which the Company's Establishments may be placed.

5th.—The Corporate Body thus constituted to be specially empowered, subject to the conditions hereafter mentioned, to carry on for and during a limited term of years (not to exceed Twenty-One Years unless under particular circumstances,) and within the Colony or Colonies specified in the Charter or Act of Incorporation, but not elsewhere, the Business of Banker; and for and during the like term to issue and circulate within the said Colony or Colonies, but in such manner only as shall not be at variance with any general Law of the Colony, Promissory Notes payable in Specie on Demand.

6th.—Such Banking Business or Issue of Notes not to commence or take place until the whole of the Fixed Capital of the Company has been subscribed for, and a moiety at least, of the Subscription paid up.

7th.—The remaining moiety of the Capital to be paid up within a given period from the date of the Charter or Act of Incorporation, such period not in general to exceed Two Years.

8th.—In all cases in which Shares in the Company's Stock are transferred between the period of the Grant of the Charter or Act of Incorporation and the actual commencing of business by the Bank, the responsibility of the original holder of the transferred Shares to continue for Six Months at least after the date of the transfer.

9th.—The Company not to advance Money on Security of Lands or Houses or Ships, or on pledge of Merchandise, nor to hold Lands or Houses, except for the transaction of its business, nor own Ships, or be engaged in Trade, except as dealers in Bullion or Bills of Exchange; but to confine its transactions to discounting Commercial Paper and negotiable Securities, and other legitimate Banking Business.

10th.—The Company not to hold Shares in its own Stock, nor to make advances on the security of those Shares.

11th.—The Discounts or Advances by the Company, on Securities bearing the name of any Director or Officer thereof, as drawer, acceptor, or endorser, not to exceed at any time one-third of the total Advances and Discounts of the Bank.

12th.—The Dividends to shareholders to be made out of Profits only, and not out of the subscribed Capital of the Company.

13th.—The total amount of the Debts and Liabilities of the Company, whether upon Bonds, Bills, Promissory Notes, or otherwise contracted, over and above the amount of Deposits on Banking Accounts with the Company's Establishments, not to exceed at any time three times the amount of the Capital Stock subscribed and actually paid up.

14th.—No Promissory or other Notes to be issued for sums under 1*l*. sterling (or in the North American Colonies 1*l*. Halifax currency), or the equivalent thereof in any other local currency, and not for fractional portions of such Pound or other equivalent amount.

15th.—All Promissory Notes of the Company, whether issued from the Principal Establishment or from Branch Banks, to bear date at the place of issue, and to be payable on demand in Specie at the place of date.

16th.—The total amount of the Promissory Notes payable on demand, issued, and in circulation, not at any time to exceed the amount of the Capital Stock of the Company actually paid up.

17th.—In the event of the assets of the Company being insufficient to meet its engagements, the Shareholders to be responsible to the extent of twice the amount of their subscribed Shares (that is, for the amount subscribed, and for a further and additional amount equal thereto).

18th.—Suspension of Specie Payments on Demand at any of the Company's Banking Establishments, for a given number of days (not in any case exceeding sixty) within any one year, either consecutively or at intervals, or other breach of the Special Conditions upon which the Company is empowered to open Banking Establishments or to issue and circulate Promissory Notes, to forfeit those privileges, which shall cease and determine upon such forfeiture as if the period for which they had been granted had expired.

19th.—The Company to make up and publish periodical Statements of its Assets and Liabilities half-yearly or yearly; showing, under the heads specified in the annexed form, the average of the amount of its Notes in circulation, and other Liabilities, at the termination of each week or month, during the period to which the statement refers, and the average amount of Specie or other Assets that were available to meet the same. Copies of these statements to be submitted to the Government of the Colony within which the Company may be established; and the Company to be prepared, if called upon, to verify such Statements by the production, as confidential documents, of the Weekly or Monthly Balance Sheets from which the same are compiled. And also to be prepared, upon requisition from the Lords Commissioners of Her Majesty's Treasury, to furnish, in like manner, such further information respecting the state or proceedings of its Banking Establishments as their Lordships may see fit to call for.

20th.—The Charter or Act of Incorporation may provide for an addition to the Capital of the Company within specified limits, with the sanction of the Lords Commissioners of the Treasury; such additional Capital, and the Shares and Subscriptions that may constitute the same, to be subject in every respect, from and after the date of the signification of such sanction, to conditions and regulations similar to those applying to the original Capital.

FORM of RETURN referred to in REGULATION No. 19.

RETURN of the Average amount of Liabilities and Assets of the Bank of , during the periods from (1st January) to (30th June) 184 , viz.:—

Liabilities.

Promissory Notes in circulation not bearing Interest . . . . . . £

Bills of Exchange in circulation not bearing Interest . . . . . . £

Bills and Notes in circulation bearing Interest . . . . £

Balances due to other banks . . . . £

Cash Deposits not bearing Interest . . £

Cash Deposits bearing Interest . . . . £

To Shareholders for Capital paid up . . . . . £

To Ditto for Additions declared to Shares (if any) £

To Ditto for Dividends remaining unpaid (if any) £

Total Average Liabilities . . . £

Assets.

Coin and Bullion . . . . £

Landed or other Property of the Corporation . . . . £

Government securities . . . . £

Promissory Notes or Bills of other Banks . . . . £

Balances due from other Banks . . . £

Notes and Bills Discounted, or other Debts due to the Corporation, not included under the foregoing heads, and exclusive of Debts abandoned as bad . . . . £

Total Average Assets . . . . £